Separation

A play

Tom Kempinski

Samuel French – London
New York – Sydney – Toronto – Hollywood

SEPARATION

First performed at Hampstead Theatre on October 14th, 1987, with the following cast of characters:

Joe Green	David Suchet
Sarah Wise	Saskia Reeves

The play was directed by **Michael Attenborough**
Designed by **Sue Plummer**

The play transferred to the Comedy Theatre, London, on December 8th, 1987 with the same cast

The action of the play takes place on a split set—the rooms of Joe, in London, and Sarah, in New York

Time: the present

SYNOPSIS OF SCENES

ACT I   SCENE 1   3 p.m. in London, 10 a.m. in New York

SCENE 2   Four weeks later. 3 a.m. in London, 10 p.m. in New York

SCENE 3   Ten days later. 2 p.m. in London, 9 a.m. in New York

SCENE 4   Three weeks later. 1 a.m. in London, 8 p.m. in New York

SCENE 5   Two weeks later. 4 p.m. in London, 11 a.m. in New York

ACT II   SCENE 1   Two months later. 4 p.m. in London, 11 a.m. in New York

SCENE 2   Three weeks later. 10 a.m. in London, 5 a.m. in New York

SCENE 3   That night. 3 a.m. in London, 10 p.m. in New York

SCENE 4   Next day

SCENE 5   Next day, morning

SCENE 6   One week later. 5.30 p.m. in London, 12.30 p.m. in New York

SCENE 7   Four months later. 1 p.m. in London, 8 a.m. in New York

DEDICATION

To the three Rs and M.A.*

To R one, who's got more balls than Sherpa Tensing

To R two, whom I lost because she lost her principles

To R three, who opened the door for this play by understanding herself

And to M.A., who is indeed a master of the arts, because he *knew* where to strip away the final lies, so I could seek the truth.

Thank you

Tom Kempinski

---

* Michael Attenborough

CHARACTERS

Joe Green Mid to late forties, playwright. Looks, if anything, a little younger than his years. Fat at the start of the play, but from Act II works his way to slimness. Lots of thick, dark hair, casual clothes, e.g. check shirts and dark trousers, though this also changes a little with light socks replacing dark ones and slippers being replaced by "trainers". Gold-rimmed spectacles, sometimes unshaven at the start of the play, but always shaven later. English.

Sarah Wise Twenty-nine to early thirties, slim, mid-length light hair, neat clothes, not expensive, but not cheap, New Yorker. No feeling in her feet makes her walk somewhat stiff-legged without crutches, but usually she uses crutches. An actress. Intelligent.

Author's Note:

On page 13 Sarah compares herself to Mary Dekker, the Olympic athlete from 1984. Directors should change this name to any other name which will be recognised by their audience, depending on which country the play is being presented in. The name should, of course, be one which an American woman would know.

T.K.

THE SET

The stage is in two parts—the two rooms of the characters—but though separated by three thousand miles, there is no wall between the two rooms, they lead into one another. **It is important that the design of the stage, usually decided before rehearsals, allows as natural a conversation at some point in the play in which the two characters are talking on the phone, but standing very near to one another.**

Joe's room is the living-room of a rented apartment/flat in north London. Some furniture is his, most is the landlord's. There is no planned design: deep wine-coloured wall-to-wall carpet; TV downstage watched all the time from a new, cheap sofa, centre; a glass-topped coffee table in front of the sofa with lots of bills, newspapers and letters on it, sometimes tidy, sometimes not. Two armchairs with covers which don't match the sofa on either side of the room—old cushions, mixed colours. A white, plastic-topped table, round, behind the sofa with an unused typewriter on it, some A4 paper and notes for unwritten plays, odd chairs round the table. Cheap book-shelves full of books, history, novels, plays, psychology, not recently read. Telephone on long wire. Door one way to bedroom, up three stairs, door other way to kitchen and exit; cuckoo clock with dramatic scene on the front. White painted walls, yellowing slightly; posters of Joe's plays and a watercolour on the walls. Shape of room irregular, half the ceiling goes higher for extra windows. Some clothes thrown over a chair. But it's not a mess, he couldn't bear it.

Sarah's room is the bedroom of a small, mid-town Manhattan highrise, twenty-third floor. Corny view of skyscrapers outside. Small room with double bed, colours rose and pale green, old furniture of style and chosen to match the room and apartment. Oriental prints and oriental lamp, thick green carpet, book-case in wall, concealed lighting, fine bedside tables matching, 'Pierre Deux' style, door to living room, telephone by bed, fine curtains held back by fine sashes.

ACT I

SCENE 1

Joe is lying on the sofa in his London apartment watching TV. It's 3 p.m. and there is a women's programme on—a female interviewer talks to a female novelist about her first novel. We can hear the interview. Joe is over-weight, unshaven, but his hair is tidy. He is eating a family-sized tin of peaches from a big bowl with a dessert spoon. He is dressed but wears slippers

Sarah sits on the bed. It's 10 a.m. in New York. Her crutches stand between the bed and the bedside table and are thus not visible. Nothing must suggest that she is ill. She sits debating with herself, because she's nervous of making the call. Finally she reaches for the phone, and dials

Joe grabs the phone on the floor next to him as it rings. He is eager for a human voice

Joe (*in a strong voice*) Hello, yes!
Sarah Hello, may I speak to a Mr Joe Green, please?
Joe (*cheerfully; on a higher note*) Yes, this is Joe Green speaking, you're Sarah Wise from New York, I can tell, there's a sort of gap and then a click, I can tell . . .
Sarah Yes, it is, I . . .
Joe (*going on*) Thanks for phoning back so quickly, you got my message on your ansaphone, right? . . .

She starts to speak again, but again he interrupts

I phoned you as soon as I got your letter via my agent this morning, I phoned at lunch, but obviously you were asleep, the five hour time difference, right?

She waits this time to make sure he's really stopped . . . He has

Sarah Yes, that's right, thank you very much for . . .
Joe (*interrupting*) Hang on a second, can you, I'm just going to switch the television off, will you hold on a second, can you wait?
Sarah (*with a chuckle*) Of course.

He gets up hastily, switches off the TV, and at the same time takes a cigarette from somewhere and lights it as he hurries back, afraid the voice might vanish. He drops on to the sofa and picks up the receiver

Joe Hello, right, yes, I've done that . . .
Sarah Right, hello . . .

He is a little more relaxed with the cigarette and the simple fact of a call, any call ...

Joe Yes. Hello, well this is nice, yes, so, I phoned straight away, as I said, I hate writing letters, never know if you're going to get an answer, much prefer the human voice, though it's loneliness of course, actually, anyway hello ...

Sarah (*laughing*) Hello again, yes, this is a human voice, I promise.

Joe Terrific, listen, how come your letter took so long to reach me, your initial letter to my New York agent was dated three months ago?

She is still a little overcome by his whirlwind opening and the fact he's a famous writer, as she sees him

Sarah Yes. Yes, I guess it has been quite a long time ...

There is at last a pause from Joe as he waits for a bit more explanation, but there is none

Joe (*finally*) Yes. I mean was there a hold up, did anyone make problems for you getting hold of me? ...

Sarah Oh, I don't think so, you have to expect these things to take a little time.

Joe Listen, you don't have to be politic with me, they probably tried to pour cold water on the whole thing, anyway you've got through to me now, well done, right, so you want to perform my play *The Empty Palate* in an off-off Broadway theatre, correct?

Sarah I'd like to do that very much, Mr Green ...

Joe Those are the little theatres in small halls and converted warehouses, right?

Sarah That's right, but they're legitimate theatres, Mr Green, I mean they're not just ...

Joe (*interrupting*) Well, you can of course perform the play there, I'll just tell my agent here and she'll draw up a contract with you ...

Sarah (*slamming her hand over the mouthpiece and exclaiming*) Oh shit, oh my God! ...

Joe has heard nothing and continues speaking over her

Joe ... Now there's one tiny problem came to me this morning, I mean don't worry, it won't stop this going ahead or anything, but ... by the way, are you rich?

Sarah has not quite recovered

Sarah Excuse me, what, I'm sorry I ...

Joe I mean is it all right for us to talk, can you afford the call, or shall I call you back?

Sarah Oh, I see, oh no, that's OK, no I'm not rich, I just do a clerical job when I'm not acting, but it's fine to go on talking, oh, Mr Green, thank you so ...

Joe (*going on*) Right. Well, my problem is ... I mean you do know the play had a run on Broadway, do you?

Sarah Oh yes, I read all the reviews, I am aware of that, of course.

Joe And then it had an off-Broadway run after that, you see . . .

Sarah Mr Green, I'm fully aware it's a successful play, I assure you we intend to treat the play very sensitively and . . .

Joe (*very tetchily*) No, no, no, it's got nothing to do with that! Look, my problem is that having had two productions with it in New York, I'm afraid that people will think I'm some kind of a megalomaniac to keep shoving my play down their throats. Can't we put something in the programme about your situation which will explain why I'm allowing the play to be put on there a third time, can we do that?

Sarah's "high" has gone. A beat

Sarah I understand what you're saying, Mr Green . . .

Joe senses her reserve and knows why

Joe Look, look, I know you actresses. You probably feel that if we state your situation in the programme people will start making allowances for you and not judge you on your merits, etc. What is your illness called, by the way?

Sarah (*from long habit, she enunciates clearly*) Relapsive . . . peripheral . . . polyneuropathy of unknown origin . . .

Joe is flippant before he can stop

Joe My God, is it as bad as it's long?!

Sarah (*cheerfully matter of fact*) Well it's pretty bad I guess, in fact it stinks.

Joe I can imagine. Are you in a wheelchair like your character in the play or on crutches or what?

Sarah had prepared herself for this question—better tell the truth

Sarah Well, I was in a wheelchair for a time after I left the hospital, but now it's just crutches outdoors and sometimes indoors too.

Joe holds off his growing realisation of her serious condition by being matter-of-fact too

Joe Yes, I see. Is it like the illness of the woman in the play? Frankly, I haven't heard of your one.

Sarah Well, hers is psychosomatic, of course. Mine's neurological, and if you want to get technical, it's progressive with remissions, though it can be acute.

Joe I'm sorry I don't quite . . .

Sarah It means you can drop dead from mine, but don't worry Mr Green, no one has ever dropped dead from it on stage, you get warnings, I promise you.

Joe (*quieter*) I see . . . I understand, well I don't understand, of course . . . (*He can't go further yet, so he goes cheerful and firm to get out of it*) Oh look, let's forget about my heightened sensibilities about what New York will think of my motives, I'll tell my agent and you just go ahead and do it.

'S' not a bad play you know, performed in over thirty countries, trumpet-trumpet, and your part's terrific . . .

It's settled, she's happy

Sarah Thank you, Mr Green, yes I know that, and thank you very, very much . . .

He goes straight on so as not to end the conversation, sitting forward on the sofa

Joe So you won't have acted for some time, I suppose, at all, is that right?
Sarah That's right. Not since my relapse seven years ago, this'll be the first time for seven years.
Joe (*quieter again*) Yes, I see. Haven't had a lot of offers to play Lady Macbeth on crutches, I suppose . . .
Sarah (*laughing*) Not too many lately, no . . .
Joe I thought not, well I hope this goes well for you.
Sarah Will you be able to come and see the production? I mean are you coming to New York on business or anything?

Joe smiles. He rises and walks round his room

Joe Sarah, the short answer is "no, I won't be coming". Now for the longer answer so you know it's not because I spit on your off-off Broadway version. I'm agoraphobic amongst other things, something to do with being sent away from my parents when I was very young, you know like those jokes about being dropped on your head when you're a baby, anyway I creep to my analyst every day in terror, I shop at the corner for food and the furthest I can get from my home is the three mile drive to Neasden, which believe me is still some considerable distance from New York . . .

Not in her wildest dreams . . .

Sarah Oh. I see.
Joe Exactly, you see, *The Empty Palate* is really about me, me, you know, the centre of the universe, in other words, and this may help you in your thespian efforts, the hysterical paralysis of your character is really a metaphor for my struggles with mental paralysis, see, that's how we do it.
Sarah (*still shocked*) Yes, I see, I mean yes, I . . . I . . .

Joe is starting to get bitter

Joe Ah yes, another little illusion shattered. I fear you probably thought I sat here all day creating dramatic works in between going to cocktail parties on the arms of screen goddesses.

She laughs out of relief at what she hopes is an opening for lighter moods

Sarah Well, to be honest, Mr Green, that's exactly what I did think!
Joe (*with some bitterness*) Take the stardust from your eyes, Ms Wise, or you'll never be a serious actress, handicapped or not. I live alone in a small flat as I have done for five years, during which time I have written

absolutely nothing. I am fat and no friends visit me, as they are powerless in the face of my determined despair . . .

Sarah (*trying a soothing interruption*) Mr Green . . .

Joe (*taking no notice, going on through her words*) I rise from a sleepless night, occasionally wash and then lie all day on my sofa and have to put up with the endless drivel of my mother. And I eat.

Sarah (*trying to apologise*) Mr Green . . .

Joe (*going right on*) And at night, for company, I take an assortment of magazines to bed. I throw them away when the pages get stuck together, if you follow me . . .

A beat

Sarah Well, they say exercise is good for you, if you're a little over-weight . . .

Her gag pulls Joe out of his inner world of anger back to the social world he's in. A beat as he recovers

Joe (*quieter*) I'm sorry. Mid-life crisis is my excuse and I'm sticking to it.

Sarah wants to make things right too

Sarah No, *I'm* sorry, I should know by now plays don't come from nowhere.

Joe sighs and shakes his head a bit

Joe (*a little down*) No, no, Ms Wise, I should be locked up . . . (*When it strikes him*) . . . which I am, of course, in a way, hmm, yes, rather good, that . . . (*His little "discovery" quite cheers him up*)

Sarah (*quieter*) Is your treatment helping, Mr Green? I mean, in the play I stay paralysed, right?

Joe has recovered his somewhat ironical good-humour

Joe Sarah, after five years of treatment I am able to inform you that the vast majority of experts in the field of human personality would now assess me as not quite, but very nearly, completely certifiably insane . . .

Sarah (*Laughing politely*) Well, you don't sound too crazy to me, Mr Green . . .

Joe (*ironic again*) It's all an act, I assure you, Ms Wise . . . (*But this nice conversation is too nice for him to bear—he has to kill it*) OK, well have a good time with it, I'm sure you'll act me brilliantly.

Sarah (*anxiously*) Oh I've done some good work before my illness came back, would you like me to send you some reviews?

Joe (*meaning what he says*) Forget it, Sarah, have a nice time with it.

Sarah Thanks very much, Mr Green. I . . . I . . . well . . .

Joe Bye, Sarah.

Sarah Goodbye, Mr Green.

They both put their phones down. Joe lies back on the sofa and looks up at the ceiling, thinking. Sarah immediately dials a number. It answers

Harold? ... It's me. Oh Harold I'm sorry to bother you at work, but I've got it, Mr Green the writer said I could do it, so I've got it, I can act! ... Thank you, Harold, I know, isn't it, take me out and let's celebrate somewhere with a special meal, will you, let's go to Marcel's? ...

There is again a pause, during which she sighs and turns her head in frustration

Harold I have waited seven years for this, they're going to have to shoot me to stop me doing this play ... No it *will* not be too tiring and I will be able to cope and *I'm* going to reserve the table at Marcel's, OK? ... (*Sarcastically*) Because it's something I can manage, Harold, I'm going to reserve the table ...

She listens for a moment again, then allows the receiver to drop into her lap for a second as she sighs again, then puts it to her ear again

(*Rather quietly*) You're going to choke me with marshmallows, did you know that? ... I can't be bothered to explain now, I want to go into the living room and just be happy, *you* book the table, Harold, pick me up, wipe my nose; I'm going now ... yes, marshmallows, I'll discuss it with you over the candles, bye.

She puts the receiver down and in the same movement pushes the phone away from her angrily

Let me breathe, you idiot ... God! ...

She leans back on her arms and her annoyance at Harold turns to happiness at being able to act after her long struggle. Suddenly, with slightly melodramatic gestures, in a low voice, to herself, alone in her room, she begins to recite a famous speech from Shakespeare

Joe sits up now, gets the phone and dials fourteen digits. It rings in Sarah's room

Sarah (*picking up the phone*) Hello?

Joe It's Joe Green from London, sorry to bother you again but I just thought, well if you want to ask anything about the play, I mean about your character or if you have any problems, do feel free to ring and ask, all right?

Sarah Oh Mr Green, that's really kind, I appreciate it.

Joe No, no, I mean you probably won't get much rehearsal time so do ... I mean what I mean is I'm not grand, so do really feel free to ring with any problems, God knows what kind of director you'll get, and so on.

Sarah Thanks Mr Green, I promise I will. Thank you.

Joe (*quieter*) I'm sorry, I was a bit abrupt just now ...

Sarah (*shyly*) That's OK ...

Joe Fine, bye then, I'll probably hear from you.

Sarah Goodbye, Mr Green.

They put the phones down again

Joe sits for a minute

Sarah takes her crutches from behind the bedside table, gets up and goes to exits with steady pace. As she goes she suddenly shakes her head and lets out the triumphant shout of the American cowboy who has successfully ridden his steer at the rodeo, raising her crutches above her head

(*Shouting*) Yee-ha!

Sarah exits

After a moment, Joe rises, goes to the TV, and just before he turns it on . . .

Joe Come on, Mother, talk to me . . .

The Lights fade to Black-Out

SCENE 2

Four weeks later

It is 3 a.m. in London, 10 p.m. in New York

Sarah's room is dark, just a shaft of light from the open door

Joe's room is dark. Suddenly the Lights go on and Joe enters in pyjamas from the bedroom. He is in terror—ancient panic sparked by a dream. He experiences a heart-rate of 140–160, difficulty breathing, the constant feeling he's going to fall over and above all the certain knowledge he's going to die NOW, which is why he keeps feeling for the pulse in his neck. He holds onto the furniture as he darts about the room

Joe Oh God . . . oh God . . . oh God . . . (*These phrases burst forth randomly. He stops somewhere, legs apart so he won't "collapse", holds his breath so he can feel the pulse in his neck . . . then resumes the impossible attempts to escape his body . . .*) But it could be . . . it could be . . . (*He goes to the window, opens it, closes it after a few deep breaths, then leaves it half-open . . . hurries to the sofa, tries to control his breathing and thus heart*)

After several more "oh Gods" he rises and hurries out to the kitchen, whence we may hear "oh God" and the click of kitchen sounds . . . and returns with a glass of milk and some biscuits

He sits on the sofa and tries to get comfort from the comfort food, but can't, so "oh God"ing, he grabs his address book from the table and, frantically in control, seeks and finds a number which he dials

Oh God . . . oh God . . . (*It answers*) Hello, hello, is that Alice Campbell, are you Alice Campbell? . . . This is Joe Green, you stage-managed my play *Dovetail* years ago, d'you remember, we met once at rehearsal, I'm fat, I'm the fat writer . . . yes I know it's three in the morning, I'm sorry, but I'm panicking, I'm afraid I'm going to die, you couldn't come over, could you, you're quite near me, eighty-six Farely Road I am, eighty-six, could you come over quickly, please? . . . I know, it is a bit odd, isn't it, look, I'm not a pervert or anything, I'm just afraid I'm going to die, couldn't you come over, please, could—I'm afraid . . . I'm just afraid I'm going to die, oh do come over, couldn't you? . . . Oh I see, yes I see, no, no, you mustn't leave them alone obviously, can't your husband look after them while you come over? . . . oh I see, yes, I'm divorced too, yes, no, no, I do see . . . (*He takes a couple of deep breaths*) God, it's a little better now anyway, could you just talk for a minute, could you just stay on the line and just talk for a little? . . . no, no, I don't need an ambulance, I'm not really going to die, well I don't know, I might be going to die, I can't tell if it's panic or real, but it's all right I'm not going to die now, don't worry, though I might be, of course, but I don't think I am anyway, how are you? . . . my heart rate goes up to about one hundred and sixty, I can't breathe, I keep thinking I'm going to fall over and I'm completely convinced I'm going to die on the spot, they call them panic attacks . . . Awful? yes, well I suppose, you're right it's certainly not as much fun as lying on a beach in Ibiza . . . though I can't get to Ibiza because I'm agoraphobic too, you see . . . no I haven't written anything since *The Empty Palate* . . . oh I just mess around, watch telly, I'm not in touch with anyone, really, except there's a little production of *The Empty Palate* going on in New York, and I talk to the actress there about her part and so on, that's about it, really . . . (*He laughs*) Well there's not much point in phoning her. She can hardly pop over here in two minutes and save me from dying, can she now, she's three thousand miles away! . . . (*Slightly sarcastically*) No, I know I'm not really dying, but you don't know that at the time you see . . . Yes, I am now, thank you, and thanks so much for putting up with me and not slamming the phone down . . . Yes, OK then, and maybe we will, you never know, bye now . . . (*He puts the phone down and just sits, taking another couple of deep breaths. Now follow a few moments of indecision— should he phone, shouldn't he? Finally he looks up the number in his address book and dials fourteen digits*)

The phone rings in Sarah's room

After a few moments Sarah enters without crutches in her dressing-gown, holding a copy of The Empty Palate

She switches on the light. She's tired and nervous about coping with acting with her handicap, yet determined to overcome all fears and difficulties. She picks up the phone and sits down on the bed

Joe acts "natural" and positive, giving no overt hint of his panic, which in any case is now less intense

Sarah Hello?
Joe (*cheerfully*) Joe Green from London again, I was passing so I thought I'd drop in.
Sarah (*tired but welcoming*) Hello, Joe Green from London again, welcome and enter.
Joe Not a bad time for you?—bit later than last time.
Sarah Not at all, I'm still up working on my lines.

Joe Ah right, so how were rehearsals today anyway?

She won't tell the writer that there are any problems for her

Sarah Oh good, everything's going really well.

Joe No, no, I mean have you any more questions, anything else I can sort out?

Sarah Well, we only spoke, what, day before yesterday, nothing new since then, really, no ... (*She yawns*) Pardon me.

Joe I'm sorry, this is too late for you, isn't it? I'd calculated ...

Sarah (*interrupting*) No, really, I'm glad you phoned, I told you, I'm still up looking at my ... (*She glances at her bedside electric clock and interrupts herself*) My God, it must be the middle of the night over there ...

Joe makes light of it

Joe Well yes, more or less, well not *exactly* the middle, when *is* the middle of the night, actually?

Sarah (*softer*) Is anything wrong, Mr Green?

Joe (*determinedly cheerful*) Wrong, Ms Wise? No, I'm just checking on my seven-per-cent-rising-to-ten-per-cent-after-recoupment, keeping you up to the mark, safeguarding my investment ...

Sarah (*laughing*) You always phone people about your seven-per-cent rising to ten-per-cent at, what, three in the morning, is that it?

He continues to cover the truth with this joke

Joe I invariably do with my overseas productions, yes, except for Poland, of course, because they won't let you take out your zlotys, but otherwise always, three a.m. regular as clockwork.

Sarah's no fool, she knows why people phone a stranger at three in the morning

Sarah It's a pity you're not writing, some writers find it good working at night, don't they?

Joe (*cheerfully*) Yes, I do ... well when I do I do, if you see what I mean? ...

Sarah Yes ... (*She yawns again from tiredness, but puts a hand over the phone to hide it from him*)

A beat

Joe Hello? ...

Sarah Yes, I'm here.

Although Joe is afraid to get too close, he nonetheless feels put off by their polite stance

Joe Listen, I'm sorry, can we drop this successful-writer-advises-minor-actress charade a little, it's like talking through an ocean of cotton wool, what's happening over there really, I'm a long way off here, you know?

She realises he wants to be a part of the play

Sarah Oh I'm sorry, I've just been so wrapped up in ... (*Crisply*) Anyway, OK, Cyrano's Diary, well, ten days into rehearsals and we're still finding our feet, s'cuse the pun, your explanations on the phone have been invaluable, since our director, as you predicted, is, well, limited, let's say, the part's just as exciting as ever and I'm propelled by complete panic.

Joe (*surprised and a bit troubled*) Panic? Why panic, did you say panic?

She didn't want to get into this

Sarah Mr Green, I didn't . . .

But since he really wants to know what's happening, she'll tell him, but very matter of factly

(*Interrupting herself*) Well OK, look, I have no feeling in my feet, right, so walking for yourself is one thing, but I worry about turning and stopping and putting things down exactly where the director wants them and stuff like that. Also it's so different acting when your body can't obey the commands you'd like to give it and then I've got some discomfort in my urethrea and . . . anyway, what should I tell you, Alicia Markova I'm not, right?

Joe is eager for the handicapped to win

Joe But you're managing though, aren't you?

Her attitude toughens even more at his hint of doubt in her

Sarah Hey, successful writer, don't get me wrong, here, I'm not managing, I'm winning, it's going to be a great show, just everyone has their own Morgan Dovid to bear.

Joe (*laughing*) So they say . . .

Sarah (*directly*) Why don't you take some sleeping pills, Joe, at least you'd get some rest.

He won't let her in

Joe (*explaining*) Well you know, I'm trying this analysis stuff and I think pills would cover things up you see.

Sarah I understand.

Joe (*eager to show it's no big thing*) Giving it a real go, as we say.

She tries another route, but lightly

Sarah Joe, I hope this isn't a stupid question, but in the play her parents send her to New York when she's two and a half for five years. She's utterly lonely, longs for them and hates them at the same time for throwing her out. In desperation she transfers her love to the foster-parents, but to her that's like killing her natural parents, result—guilt, seeds of self-loathing, etc., all buried, which erupts when she meets a parallel situation in adult life. My stupid question is, if you know so much about yourself, how come you're not well yet?

He's embarrassed—she's found him out and asked a direct question, but, caught by surprise, he answers directly

Joe Because it's not just a question of knowing generally; it's a question of re-experiencing each detail.

Sarah (*gentler*) I understand.

He retreats again into the play

Joe (*clearing his throat*) Well, if there's nothing else, I'll leave you to get on
  . with your lines, you're quite sure there's nothing else, nothing else I can
  sort out.
Sarah Not right now, but thanks, but I'm sure there will be as we go on,
  anyway.
Joe Right, yes, absolutely, well, goodnight.
Sarah (*kindly*) Goodnight, I hope you can get some sleep now.
Joe Oh, good God, bound to, no problem, goodnight. (*In the instant before
  putting his phone down, he senses she's still holding on*) Hello? ...
Sarah Joe, if you want to phone anytime, I mean just for a chat or
  whatever, that's OK, I'm home all the time now, I mean at night.

He still has to hold her at a distance

Joe Oh well, that's very decent, but we'll be talking regularly about the play
  anyway, won't we?

*She begins to want to explain that that wasn't what she meant, but in that
instant senses his reserve and changes her words*

Sarah That's right. Well thanks again, goodnight.
Joe Goodbye ... (*Correcting himself automatically*) Goodnight.

Both put their receivers down, and think for a moment

The Lights fade to Black-Out

SCENE 3

Ten days later

It is 2 p.m. in London and 9 a.m. in New York

*Joe's room is empty. Sarah is asleep in her bed. A beat. Then her electric alarm
goes off. She wakes and turns it off, lies there a moment because she's very
tired, but also wants to get up, so she rubs her face a little, reaches for her
crutches, gets up and exits to freshen up*

*Some noise as Joe enters his apartment, appearing immediately in the living
room dressed in slippers and a donkey jacket and carrying two plastic shopping
bags. He goes straight to the TV and switches it on—a quiz show—then exits
to put the shopping away in the kitchen*

*Sarah returns on crutches, gets back into bed, shakes her head to wake fully,
then takes the phone and dials. It rings in Joe's room. He waddles in fast, still
in his jacket, rushes to turn off the TV and grabs the phone. He is expecting
Sarah's call*

Joe Hello, yes? Sarah? ...

Sarah (*excited through her tiredness*) Joe, we were a hit, it was perfect, Joe, perfect! . . .

Joe Of course you were a hit, you were performing a brilliant play! . . .

Sarah Not the play, dummy, us! The production, me, us! . . .

Joe My coaching and advice via numerous extremely expensive phone-calls have obviously paid off . . .

Sarah Have you ever had a lightweight aluminium crutch wrapped round your head, Green? . . .

Joe (*chuckling*) Not lately. Listen, I'm only kidding, well done, congratulations.

Sarah (*full of enthusiasm*) Joe, they applauded for so *long*, and my parents flew over from Brussels and was my father proud, he nearly burst out of his tuxedo! . . . (*Calming a little into gratitude*) Joe, it was really good . . .

Joe Sarah, I'm absolutely delighted for you, listen, did you really fee . . .

Sarah (*sitting up and interrupting*) Oh my God, I nearly forgot. The director of a little theatre in San Francisco was in and listen to this, he wants to take the show to his theatre! . . . (*Anxiously*) Can I do it, Joe, are the rights available, he asked me, oh Joe, tell me they are? . . .

Joe (*somewhat surprised*) I didn't realise you could get to San Francisco I mean, you know, I had the . . .

Sarah (*interrupting*) Sure I can, I don't have to walk, you know, we have these things called aeroplanes over here and . . .

Joe (*interrupting*) Yes, yes, yes, I know that, I meant . . . Anyway yes the rights are available and of course you can do it and that's wonderful, so listen have you really got her character now, I mean did . . .

Sarah (*interrupting, cheerfully appalled*) Joe, I have just opened the play to the thunderous applause of sixty of New York's most discriminating theatre-goers, you phoned me practically every other day, I do, yes, *fully* understand her, yes I do.

Joe Ah yes, but I don't mean just understand her in words, I mean in the *bone*, in the *marrow*, *that's* "understand", *not* "I understand, Joe, I understand", I mean has she really become a part of you, that's what I mean by "understand".

A beat

Sarah (*gentler*) 'Cos it's you, isn't it?

Joe What is me?

Sarah Oh, come on Joe, in the play, being sent to New York for five years in the war, blaming herself, turning rage into self-destruction, she's you, right, you said so, Joe.

Joe Sarah, render unto Sigmund the things that are Sigmund's and unto art etc. etc., we are talking here about the play.

Sarah (*taking his sentence on*) Which is you . . .

Joe Listen, young lady, one of my plays a few years back was about a mother/son relationship, and in the Belgian production they set the whole thing in a womb, you know womb, the whole set, the full bit, fallopian tubes, ovaries, for all I know the entrance at the back of the stage was the vagina, now look, listen . . .

He pauses as Sarah is roaring with laughter. He laughs with her a little then speaks when she has recovered

I'm telling you, it's true. Look I'm three thousand miles away here, how can I really know if you've understood her?

Directly and without bitterness, Sarah gives it to him straight

Sarah Joe I first caught this shitty disease when I was thirteen. When it came back seven years ago, I nearly died. My parents stood over my bed and looked very sad and I hated them because they were going to live and I wasn't. So this *young lady* understands the dynamics of separation *old man*, in the bone and in the marrow ...

Joe (*appalled and frightened*) But I didn't know you nearly d ... d ... that you almost died, you didn't say that, you've never said that ...

Sarah (*laughing*) That's because all you'd ever discuss was the lousy friggin' play!

Joe (*pursuing his own thoughts*) I thought you just had some kind of paralysis and that was it. I mean how are you then really? ...

Sarah Joe for the first time in seven years I've been thinking about "life-problems", getting to rehearsals, my character, not doctor's waiting-rooms and *death*, the condition is stable, it may stay that way or not, but I'm working, that's how I am ...

Joe (*quieter*) Yes, I see ...

Sarah (*cheerfully*) Listen, I've got funny insides and my legs don't work too well. You wrote a play about me, remember? What did you expect, Mary Dekker?

Joe (*in a Humphrey Bogart voice*) Listen, you shtick wid me, kid, we're a team, from now on you act exshclushively in my plays, I can ficsh it for you sho you're in a bed or on crutches or in a wheelchair, right.

Sarah (*cheekily*) You like your women a little crippled, don't you?

Joe (*politely outraged*) I *beg* your pardon?!

Sarah You guys who're afraid of vaginas, you like us a little crippled, don't you, makes us less scary, less chance of getting it bitten off, right?

Joe And who says I was afraid of vaginas, may I ask, what's going on here, I've been married!

Sarah Well, put it this way, you're not going out on the arms of any screen-goddesses, are you, that much we *do* know! ...

Joe Listen, Greta Garbo, I know you still have the applause of sixty of America's most discriminating theatre-goers ringing in your ears, but how come you're so cheeky today, you eaten too many oysters or something?

Sarah As a matter of fact, just the opposite. I've stopped eating so many marshmallows, I was choking on marshmallows, so I just cut them right out ...

Joe (*suddenly grumpy*) Well, I don't know what you're talking about at all, all I said was that I'd write some plays for you that took account of your handicap, but since I can't even write I can't give them to you anyway, so

I don't know how you get from that to me liking crippled women, or whatever you meant . . .

Sarah puts on a perfect Noel Coward tone and accent, rolling the "r" in "grand" and "dearest"

Sarah Joe, dearest, we're having our first tiff, isn't it grrrand! . . .
Joe (*wryly*) Wonderful . . .
Sarah (*in her own voice*) Joe, this is yuk, but I have to say it.
Joe I'm sorry, what's yuk, what do you mean?
Sarah (*interrupting*) I . . . I'm sending you something.
Joe (*surprised*) Oh? . . .?
Sarah (*interrupting*) I'm sending you a little silver statue of Joe Louis . . .
Joe (*laughing*) You're what?! . . .
Sarah (*a little embarrassed*) Yeah, I know. Anyway it's a little six-inch high statue of Joe Louis in silver, my father put it next to me in hospital when I was dying, you know, kind of symbol of the big fight-back etc., etc., and it's really ghastly—
Joe (*beginning to be touched*) Sarah . . .
Sarah (*going straight on*) . . . the guy who sculpted these things is an ex-convict who went to jail for twenty years for multiple rape and while he was in jail he reformed and learnt to sculpt and became a human being and blah, blah, blah, you know, one of *those* stories, anyway if his "Joe Louis" period is anything to go by he should have stuck to multiple rape, believe me, anyway, I've sent it . . .

Joe ignores her jokey "cover" and is very moved

Joe (*quietly*) Thank you very much . . .
Sarah (*off-hand*) Yeah well, my mother always said if you say thank you it'll guarantee a trouble-free path through life, which of course is how it turned out for me, as you know . . .

A beat. Joe changes tack to hesitantly ask the question he's wanted to ask for some time

Joe (*quieter*) Sarah, if . . . if you can go with the play to San Francisco, see I didn't realise you could travel, so, well would you like to drop by here, I mean, well would you feel like popping over here for a visit, say? . . .
Sarah (*sighing and blowing out her cheeks*) Shit, Joe, I thought you'd never ask . . .
Joe (*very English; surprised*) I beg your pardon?
Sarah I thought I was going to have to invite myself over there . . .
Joe Well, it's only becau . . .
Sarah (*going on*) . . . these last few calls I've been like a teenager on her tenth date with some guy who just talks and talks and all she wants is to make out with him . . .
Joe Oh . . .
Sarah OK, OK, don't panic, I'm not going to leap on you. Of course I want to come and see you, what kind of person do you think I am?
Joe Well, I just didn't know if physically, you know, whether . . .

Sarah (*interrupting*) Well, I can physically and I want to come.

Joe (*inevitable*) Well, why do you want to come anyway?

Sarah I don't believe this, I'm not hearing this, you gave me a start, Green, you gave someone a leg up who doesn't have any legs, I'm born again, I'm the only born-again Jew in New York ... anyway I like you ...

Joe (*beginning to be angry*) What d'you mean you like me, you've never even met me ...

Sarah Well, I like you and I'm coming over.

Joe Sarah this is a fantasy, you're making a fantasy out of me, how can you like what you don't know?

Sarah I *do* know and I think you're nice and there's a specialist over there who understands my illness so I'm coming, next question.

Joe, through fear, is by now really angry

Joe Well I am not "nice", to use your shallow term. I *am* a fat, middle-aged, insane pudding, that is what I am, and there is nothing "nice" about it! ...

She senses his fear and reins back

Sarah (*a shade quieter*) Joe. Do you think you're Napoleon?

Joe (*angrily*) No of course I don't thin ...

Sarah (*interrupting*) D'you think you're a scrambled egg, and walk around scared people are going to eat you and sprinkle pepper on you? ...

He cannot help beginning to laugh through his anger

Joe Look, that is not the poi ...

Sarah (*interrupting*) Then you're not insane.

Joe But I *am*, that is precisely wha ...

Sarah (*interrupting again*) No you're not and I'm coming over to see you and it's *not* a fantasy, I like you and I'm not going to discuss it. (*She begins to puff up her pillows and smooth her bedcover in preparation to going back to sleep*)

Joe (*the rational man*) Sarah. It is a lot more complicated than just ...

When she has finished organising her bedclothes, she settles back onto her pillow

Sarah Joe, I'm very tired and I have relapsing peripheral puke and I have a long show tonight and for two more weeks and then San Francisco and then I'm going to be doing this show for the rest of my life, because there aren't any other plays I can do, so I'm getting into training for a very long run, so goodbye.

Joe God, Sarah, I wish I could write for you ...

Sarah is now settled comfortably back on her pillows

Sarah Don't worry about writing, we'll get you writing, we'll discuss it when I see you. Goodbye. (*She turns on to her side, ready to sleep*)

Joe (*not letting it go*) Sarah, you don't ... Look. I hardly ever brush my teeth, hardly *ever*, *and* I won't go to the dentist and I use roll-on deodorant if I haven't washed for a bit and sometimes I just sit in a chair

and do nothing and feel as if my head's full of concrete and I'm very bitter
and angry, don't you see, I'm a mess, I'm not this polite voice you hear on
the phone, I'm a mess! ...

Sarah (*cosily*) D'you know a good hotel over there that's not too expensive?

Joe (*exasperated*) Sarah! Will you come down off your high because the play
went well and *listen*, I'm attempting to give you a truthful picture of ...

Sarah jerks up on to her elbow. She is very firm

Sarah Green! Relapsive peripheral puke has not made me deaf, I did hear
you invite me over to see you, didn't I, this is true, this happened, right!?

Joe Yes, of course it happened, I'm onl ...

Sarah (*interrupting; loudly*) Then why're you making it sound as if I'm
coming over there to a re-run of Hiroshima!!?

Joe I'm not, I'm simply ...

Sarah (*interrupting; soothing*) Joe. I'm not coming over there to marry you,
my father will not be behind me with a shot-gun insisting we tie the
conjugal knot because I said "vagina" to you on the phone ... I'm
coming to visit a friend, you know, like the milkman but a bit longer.
Right, now all I want is for you to say, "Sarah Wise, I want you to visit
me," just say that and we'll both know what's going on, OK?

Joe Sarah of *course* I want you to v ...

Sarah (*interrupting; firmly*) Good. Wonderful, now screw off, hang up, go
away, your artistic temperament is keeping me awake ... (*she flops her
head on to the pillow*)

Joe (*shouting quickly in case Sarah hangs up*) So when are you coming, when,
Sarah, you haven't said!?

Sarah (*sleepily*) Either straight after this run in New York, or after San
Francisco, depends when it is, bye Joe.

Joe I'll tell my agent to OK the San Francisco contract when it comes
through, ... 'bye.

*He waits, but there is no response because Sarah has let her arm with the
receiver fall on to the bed—she's nearly asleep*

(*Softly*) Sarah? ...

*He puts down his own receiver very gently, then walks to the TV, is about to
turn it on, then doesn't—he's beginning to feel he doesn't need it. Cheerfully he
insults the television*

Load of rubbish ...

He exits to hang up his jacket, muttering a song

The Lights fade to Black-Out

SCENE 4

Three weeks later

It's 1 a.m. in London, 8 p.m. in New York

Joe and Sarah are talking on their phones, Joe lying on the sofa, relaxed, Sarah sitting on the bed, eating an apple, relaxed too. There is a bottle of aspirin and a glass of water on her bedside table to help with recent sharp discomfort in her urethrea. Lights low, though not dim

Joe ... no, the thing about Brando is that he does show feelings, whereas Olivier wants to *master* feelings, he shows the *domination* of feelings, that's the essential difference, I think ...

Sarah (*through her apple*) But those are feelings too, in a way, aren't they?

Joe (*thinking*) Well it's ... I think what I mean is that with Brando you always get this sense of something *behind* what he's saying, God I know this sounds corny but the human condition is always in there somewhere, I think that's what I mean ...

Sarah (*just enjoying the conversation*) I'll give you my considered opinion when I've finished this apple.

Joe Do you go to the movies much, are you a movie buff?

Sarah Yes, I'm going again now, but I'm not fanatic, just your average movie-goer, I guess.

Joe And theatre, do you go to the theatre much?

Sarah Oh God, yes, whenever I can, oh sure.

Joe (*fractionally hesitant*) Do you go alone, with friends, you have to take a friend, do you?

Sarah suddenly has a sharp pain in her lower abdomen, which makes her say "Ow" and rub the spot with her hand

Sarah? ...

She goes on rubbing her side, but betrays nothing in her voice

Sarah It's OK, I just hit my elbow on the bed.

Joe (*suspecting nothing*) Oh ... No, I was just asking how does going to the theatre work out, you have to go with a friend, do you, I mean to help you physically, probably?

Her discomfort and his evasiveness make her very direct

Sarah I'm not a virgin, Joe.

Joe Oh, no ...

Sarah (*interrupting*) And I enjoy sex.

Joe Yes. Right. Sarah! ...

Sarah (*going on*) Now that should tell you that I have had relationships, but I should add that there is no-one special at this precise moment.

Joe Sarah, why are you telling ... ?

Sarah (*going on*) I think that gives you all the information you're seeking behind those little "so-you-go-to-the-theatre-with-friends" type questions, doesn't it?

Joe (*embarrassed*) Er, yes, I think, er, yes it does ...

Sarah Terrific.

Her pain has eased, but not completely gone. Joe is upset. A beat

Joe (*down*) Sarah ...
Sarah (*still sharp*) What!?
Joe You're angry about San Francisco, aren't you?
Sarah (*looking to the heavens*) Joe, we've been over all of this, I'm not angry about San Francisco.
Joe (*down*) But you are. Aren't you, that's the real reason you haven't been over to see me, isn't it?
Sarah Joe, I told you, I just had to have a couple of routine check-ups, just two appointments I had to keep that's all, it's medical.
Joe So you are still coming?
Sarah Of course I'm coming, I said I was coming so I'm coming, relax, we just have to wait for the results of the tests.
Joe How long will that be now?
Sarah (*kindly*) Soon, Joe, they never take that long, really.

But he feels guilty and can't let go. A beat

Joe (*down*) But you are upset about San Francisco, aren't you?
Sarah (*insistent, with a half-laugh*) I'm not upset about San Francisco! ...
Joe But I *know* how much you wanted to *do* it ...
Sarah Can we close the chapter, please, you get dozens of requests to do the play, I absolve you, not guilty.
Joe But I should have checked when I got a request for a production of the play in San Francisco that it was *your* production, by not checking I'm responsible for you not doing it and someone *else* doing it there ...

Her worry about the pain and the truth of what he says makes her suddenly snap

Sarah (*angrily*) OK, you messed up San Francisco for me, you've ruined my life, I'm in total despair and I never want to see you as long as I live, is that what you wanted to hear, you feel better now!!?
Joe (*mumbling*) Sorry ...

Now she in turn is down, worried. A beat

Sarah Joe, let's be careful, can we? ...
Joe What do you mean?
Sarah You're my friend, right?
Joe Yes, of course I'm your friend ...?
Sarah (*interrupting*) And I don't just mean for giving me the play. When I said just now there was no-one special that doesn't apply to you, you *are* special to me now, OK?
Joe (*not understanding*) Sarah, you're special to me too, why? ...
Sarah (*interrupting him; sharply*) No! ... (*Firmly*) I mean where you feel hollow and bitter and empty, those are places I can breathe and exist, when we talk you have room for me, and I need that, I need it, you understand me?
Joe (*quietly*) I know ...

Sarah (*a little softer*) OK then, just don't turn against me.

Joe (*appalled, he doesn't understand*) Turn against you, what on earth are you *talking* about!? . . .

Sarah (*low*) Don't be too grabby, Joe . . .

Joe (*the word is unfamiliar*) Don't be too *what*?

Sarah (*still low*) Don't be too grabby, don't grab, Joe.

Joe (*understanding*) Sarah! Oh, my God, oh look, I know I'm over-demanding for God's sake, that's all come to light in the last years, but by understanding it I can more and more deal with it, I can handle it, truly! . . .

She doesn't believe him really

Sarah (*neutral*) OK. . . .

Joe (*hearing her disbelief*) Sarah, I can! . . .

Sarah (*still not believing him, of course*) OK, then . . .

Joe I am *telling* you I *can*! . . .

Pause

Sarah Joe, I don't know if you're more scared of me coming or more scared of me not coming, but when I get there, let me breathe, OK.

She's hit the nail on the head, so he makes a big gag as a cover

Joe Sarah, I will open all the windows, I will open all the doors, I will obtain one of those tools whose name escapes me which bores holes in brick walls, you will be sitting in Emmenthal cheese here, the draughts will be like a typhoon, breathing, Sarah, is my main talent! . . .

Just as he finishes his speech, her pain returns quite badly. She's not doubled-up completely, but it's bad enough for her to lean into the pain and not be able to speak as she rubs her side, so there is a pause from her where Joe is expecting her to answer. He waits a moment

(*Finally*) Sarah? . . .

She gives no hint of the problem, but instead makes an excuse to get a few moments on her own

Sarah My door-bell's rung—it'll be the electrician, there's a little problem; can you hold on a second?

Joe Oh, of course . . .

He holds on, as Sarah puts the receiver under a pillow so he won't hear any grunts, lies back, trying to ease the pain with her hand and curling up a little

Sarah Shit, little discomfort, you're getting to be a real pain . . .

A beat. Joe sits, rubs his hands, then rubs his tired face, then looks at his watch

The Lights fade to Black-Out

SCENE 5

Two weeks later. Sunday

It is 4 p.m. in London, 11 a.m. in New York

Joe is lying on the sofa in pyjamas and a dressing gown, reading the Sunday papers. A portable radio plays Mozart on the table next to him. He shows no sign of weight-loss

Sarah is also sitting in her dressing gown on the end of her bed. She is nervous about phoning, but has to

The Mozart plays, beautiful. The sun shines into both rooms . . . Sarah dials. It rings in Joe's room. He finishes a line, turns the radio down and answers the phone. He's very relaxed

Joe Hi, is that you?

Sarah Yes, hi.

Joe Hi.

Sarah Finished your lunch yet?

Joe I have indeed, I'm reading the Sundays.

Sarah And may I enquire, without any hint of pressure, what you ate?

Joe (*proudly*) Two ounces of cottage cheese, two slices of bread, weighed, a teaspoon of margarine, four ounces orange juice, tea with saccharin and skimmed milk . . .

Sarah Joe! I won't recognise you!

Joe How, as Alice once enquired, can you *not* recognise me when you have never recognised me?

Sarah Oh I know, but you know what I mean . . .

Joe Yes. Yes indeed when you come over you will be meeting the "Invisible Man", yes indeed.

Sarah See, you said you'd do it and you have.

Joe continues in his positive mood

Joe Yes, well that's all very well for you to say sitting over *there*, but you're going to be costing me a fortune in new clothes when I'm slim, you know that, don't you?

Sarah *I'm* going to be costing you!? . . .

Joe Well, you don't think I'm enduring this horrendous deprivation of my tinned peaches and macaroni cheese for myself, do you, I'm only doing this so we don't get jammed in my living room door when we try to get through it side-by-side! . . .

Sarah (*laughing*) Can you see your whatsit over the horizon yet, or do you still have to look in a full-length mirror?

Joe Mind your own business! If you must know, if I bend very far forward I'm just starting to catch sight of the end of it *without* using a mirror, so there!

She laughs

Anyway, what are you doing today? Going out with one of your non-special friends, or having one round to tea, or are you just *having* one? . . .

She picks this moment to "confess" her dangerous news, which she utters fearfully but abruptly, with pretended normality

Sarah (*quietly*) I've got a part in a play, Joe . . .
Joe (*sitting up*) What!
Sarah (*quietly*) I've got a part in a play, I've been rehearsing a week . . .
Joe Sarah, this is brilliant, what is it, how did you get it, why haven't you mentioned it before?! . . .

She is careful, afraid of his response

Sarah It's a Tennessee Williams play, *Small Craft Warnings*, course it's not one of his major plays . . .
Joe But this is brilliant, what's the part, is it good, I don't know it? . . .
Sarah (*still carefully*) Well, it's not a big part, actually, but it's a real part, you know, and it's off-Broadway this time, so that's quite nice too . . .
Joe Sarah, this is like a dream-come-true for you, but is she in a wheel-chair, is she on crutches, what's the deal?

Sarah's still nervous, cautious

Sarah That's what's so nice, I guess, she's neither, they just gave me the part and said the crutches would be fine.
Joe (*with quiet joy*) This is absolutely extraordinary . . .
Sarah (*quietly*) Be happy for me, Joe, 'cos guess what, I got the role from *The Empty Palate*. I didn't audition, they just saw me and chose me, so I got it from you anyway . . .
Joe Be happy for you, what have I been saying, for Christ's sake, it's just . . . it's wonderful . . .
Sarah It's good, isn't it? . . .
Joe It is indeed very, very good, Sarah . . .

Pause. Still not secure about his real reactions, Sarah picks something "cheerful". Joe doesn't hear anything she says, as happiness and pain interpenetrate and transform inside him

Sarah God, Joe, I have to laugh. There's rather a steep iron staircase where we rehearse and naturally some of the actors offer to help me up and down, but I say "no" and tackle it myself, of course it would be absolutely *reasonable* of me to accept their help, I do have a handicap right, but I so much want to be independent, I over-compensate, d'you know what I mean, do you have that?

Joe, in his own thoughts, gets up and walks to the edge of his room near hers

Joe You do realise, you're on your way, you've crossed over into ordinary life, out of the handicapped life, I mean that's what this means . . .

She senses from his not answering her that what she fears may be near

Sarah Well, I don't know, you'd have to say tha . . .
Joe (*going on*) I mean directors who see you in the play won't know you use crutches yourself, of course they'll find out when they offer you a job, but

by then some will take you anyway, I mean this could lead to regular work, you know, just natural living . . .

Sarah Oh come on, one rose doth not a summer make, right, the industry's not . . .

Joe's apparent excitement for her and his common-sense explanations now become increasingly filled and taken over by bitterness

Joe No, no, but it does, that's what it means, it does, you'll be up and away getting work, going to auditions with your non-special friends, reminding directors of the success you had with *The Empty Palate*, and the old, fat fart who set the whole thing in motion will soon be forgotten along with the heart-felt protestations of special feelings and all the rest of the fraudulent nonsense, of course; which is why you haven't been over to see me as soon as you got some tiny part in an eminently forgettable play, right? . . .

Sarah gets up, frightened and horrified and now stands near the side of her room next to Joe's—they are very close

Sarah Joe, I told you it's purely medical reasons which have kept . . .

He interrupts, sarcastically, but still holding back the final wave of rage

Joe Oh, come on, come on, happens all the time, people do your plays, they *love* the part, they *love* the play, they come over to tea for chats about the character, they reveal little bits of themselves to ingratiate themselves with you—the writer who gives them life—but actually they conceal everything; they pretend love, they conceal mere need. The play opens, it's a flop or a hit, down comes the shutter, you never see them again, and if you meet again by chance, you're strangers. Aren't I right, are you saying it's not so? . . .

Fear makes her voice a little shrill

Sarah I'm saying that with us it's different, with us it's very, very . . .

Forty-five years of bitterness and feelings of betrayal erupt out of Joe

Joe Oh please! Don't bleed all over me, OK, we're not in the operating theatre now, you're going to bugger off like all the rest of them, you've had your pound of flesh, you've sucked the old carcass dry, so now the carrion crow moves on to corpses new, oh yes, true to form, my bird, true to type. You, of course, can act while I can't write, so I am left once again to sit on my slowly thinning arse and contemplate the wreck of my life and wonder why I persist and persist and persist in choosing faithless, phoney women who begin by showering me with their most ardent displays of affection and love and then throw me out like a dead dog over a cliff, *that*, doctor, is the little problem we must spend the *next* forty years or so looking into, don't you think, wouldn't you say so, eh doc, hmm . . . (*Roaring*) WELL, WOULDN'T YOU SAY SO, SARAH!!!? . . .

Sarah has been standing rigid during this outburst. There is a beat. Suddenly she gives vent to her own real situation for the first time. The outburst is not hysteria. It is controlled but very strong, oil gusher from the depths

Sarah You bastard!, you absolute bastard! . . .

Joe is rigid, open-mouthed

I'm in PAIN again, and it could be a relapse and I don't know if it is and the doctor doesn't know and I didn't want to load it onto you, so I didn't tell you and *THAT's* why I haven't been to see you yet, you *bastard*, and I didn't come to you and say I'd make you happy, I didn't come and say I'd give you peace, love and paradise, I phoned you up for the play, I came for the God-damn play and I said so. I was straight with you, I've always been straight with you, you bastard, and then we *did* become friends, we *did*, and you became . . . you became . . . (*She is on the point of crying, but won't show him, because she wants to stay angry, so she shouts loudly*) MY DOOR BELL'S RINGING, YOU STAY THERE, YOU HEAR ME, YOU STAY THERE!!

As Joe stands rigid with shock and shame she puts her hand over the mouthpiece and holds it to herself, bending forward slightly with the phone clasped to her middle. She tightens her mouth to hold back the tears, though a few get through . . .

Bastard . . . Bastards . . . (*She sits on the bed and when she feels she has the sorrow-part sufficiently under control, she continues, just as angry but a little more controlled putting the phone back to her mouth*)

Yes, we heard a lot about your problems, Joe, and I know you're struggling, I know you're trying to get out from under, but it takes two to tango, my friend, so let me *tell* you about my male friends you're always making snidey enquiries about, because from thirteen when I had my first attack I have needed strong men, Joe, strong doctors to save my life and a strong father to wheel me around, and I was just a body, I was just the victim and they did all the living for me. And then when the attack passed in my teens I was still afraid to stand up for myself in case the promised relapse came and I needed the strong men again, so I never stood up to my father, I never tangled with him so I was no use to him at all, I was his girl, but I wasn't the girl he wanted . . . (*Quieter*) And then I became a woman, and I went out with strong men and kept my mouth shut. And then seven years ago I *did* have the big relapse and after I got better, that is after I got out of hospital a semi-basket case, the strong and capable men stood in line to look after me . . . (*Shouting*) but they weren't strong men! they weren't, they were the screw-the-rubber-doll brigade, they wanted to help me upstairs and into cars and run my life but (*she rises*) God help me if I suggested which restaurant to go to or any other sign of independence, because they *wanted* me weak, that's what they *liked* about me, they *liked* my *miserable illness* . . . (*Quietly*) and then I met you, Joe. (*Shouting*) And you needed me, you need me, you big, dumb bastard, you need me desperately, you stupid ass-hole! . . . (*She stops, breathless, but*

goes on soon, driven by her need for him. Quieter) Yes. You needed me.
And suddenly I was a somebody after all. Some poor, screwed-up,
intelligent, funny writer needed me ... *(Shouting)* because I kept you
going on the end of this God-damn phone, I kept you out of desperation
and that is a *valuable deed ... (Quietly, matter-of-fact)* and what do you
do, you deliberately screw-up San Francisco for me in some childish
attempt to stop me getting away, *(with a half-laugh)* when I didn't want to
get away at all. I was coming after you ...

She pauses, and Joe weakly starts an excuse

Joe I don't think I ...

Sarah *(interrupting, shouting)* You shut up, you shut up, you liar, you listen!
... *(Deliberately)* You screwed up San Francisco for me to try and keep
me, and now I've got this new play you say, "I give you a choice, Sarah
Wise, stay in the rubber-doll-paralysed necrophilia league and I accept
you, or be the struggling-to-be-a-human-being type and I throw you
out ..." *(Shouting)* Well, you will stop this! You will stop this immediately now, you need me and you will let me help you and mean something
and help you write and have my place, you absolute, total complete
utter bastard!! ... *(She stops, completely drained, panting)*

*Joe is almost completely paralysed, trapped between his hatred of her
"freedom" and his despair at losing her. But his fear of losing her and genuine
love and affection just win on balance, so he can just speak after a long pause*

Joe *(quiet and strangled)* I am ... I am of course ... I am of course ... *(He
grinds to a halt)*

Sarah speaks through her heavy breathing after a moment

Sarah It's OK, Joe, it's OK ...

*The infinitesimal encouragement of her talking gets him started again after a
beat*

Joe ... I am of course conscious ... of your situation ... *(He stops again)*
Sarah *(quieter)* It's OK ...
Joe I couldn't have written the play without ... I have of course felt ...
your ... pain ...
Sarah *(gentle through her still hard breathing)* I know ... I know you did ...
Joe But it's ... an old, an ancient wound ... I thought ... I'd hoped it was
almost healed ...

There is a long, long pause. Sarah has recovered slightly. Joe stands still

Sarah Yeah, I know ...
Joe Yes ...

They remain thus, joined and separated by so much. Pause

The Lights fade to Black-Out

ACT II

SCENE 1

Two months later

It is 4 p.m. in London, 11 a.m. in New York

Joe enters his room with a vacuum cleaner. He is visibly slimmer and, because he still wears his "fat" clothes, his trousers and shirt balloon somewhat. He also wears trainers for the first time. He plugs in the vacuum cleaner and starts to hoover the room, tidying plates and clothes as he goes

Sarah enters her room in day clothes. Her mood is firm, her tone to Joe at the start is one of understanding sarcasm. Setting her crutches down on the bed next to her, she sits and dials. The phone rings in Joe's room. He finishes a bit more hoovering, switches off the machine and picks up the phone. He does not expect Sarah, so his opening word is quite open and neutral

Joe Hello?

Sarah (*a slight sigh*) Hello ...

Joe sits carefully in a chair as he answers, as if he must tread delicately

Joe Hello ...

Sarah (*ironically*) Nice to hear you're still alive. How are you?

Joe (*quietly*) I'm fine, thank you.

Sarah (*firmly*) Good. I'm glad to hear it.

A beat as she makes him speak

Joe (*mouse-like*) How are you, Sarah?

Sarah I'm fine. And I'm here.

Joe (*mouse-like*) Yes. I'm glad.

Sarah What I mean is, as you can hear, I did not abandon you.

Joe I know. Thanks.

Sarah I did the play which was not yours and I met lots of people in sweaty jeans and one with a fur coat and two who were very handsome and I discussed character and motivation with them and not with you ...

Joe (*quietly*) Yes, I ...

Sarah (*going on*) And *despite* doing this play which was *not* yours with these handsome people, two of whom wanted to help me into cars and one of whom wanted to help himself into me, despite *all* this, I am now talking to you and not one of them, correct?

Joe (*quietly*) Yes, thank ...

Sarah (*going on*) . . . I *could* have been on the phone to one of them, I even
  seriously considered it, but I'm not, so what does that make you realise?
Joe (*quietly*) It proves you haven't abandoned me . . .
Sarah Exactly, it does, doesn't it?
Joe Yes . . .
Sarah So your rather unoriginal theory about how all women betray you
  will now have to be re-adjusted, won't it?
Joe (*humbly*) Yes, it will . . .
Sarah Yes, it will, because there is at least one exception to it, isn't there,
  who is that?
Joe (*humbly*) You . . .
Sarah Correct.
Joe (*humbly*) Thank you . . .
Sarah Don't mention it, and thanks a lot for phoning so regularly and
  asking how the play was going . . .

She stops. His turn

Joe (*quietly*) Sarah, I'm sorry I haven't phoned, I . . .
Sarah (*interrupting*) Don't even think about it, I now realise that sending
  you away to America when you were two-and-a-half was undoubtedly a
  mistake on my part . . .
Joe (*laughing a little*) Yes that was a slight miscalculation, I think . . .
Sarah Anyway, I couldn't phone you either, so we're even, let's forget it.

Joe is now a little more cheerful

Joe Listen, no-one sent *you* away when *you* were two-and-a-half, what's
  your excuse?
Sarah My reasons are a little more conventional, I just hated your guts . . .

Joe is very happy and laughs

Joe Yes, I see, yes that is rather boring and uncomplicated isn't it . . .
Sarah I'll try and work in some more anguish next time, I know how
  comfortable you are with it . . .

He lets it go, serious again

Joe (*quietly*) Sarah, I thought about you a lot . . .
Sarah I know.
Joe (*insisting; as if she had denied it*) No, but I did, and I would have phoned
  but, I was afrai . . . I couldn't, (*Suddenly enthusiastic*) but listen, I have
  something very important to tell you . . .

She thinks it's more apology

Sarah Joe, it's OK, really. I was angry too for a while and then I was
  running around between doctors anyway, so why don't we just . . .
Joe (*very upset; interrupting*) Oh, Sarah . . .
Sarah Turn the page, OK?
Joe (*insisting*) Yes, but I knew you were in pain, you *told* me and I just left
  you! I . . .

Sarah (*interrupting*) Joe, we nearly blew it, OK, but in the end we didn't, so we're smart, right?

Joe Yes, but we have to find out *why* we nearly blew it, otherwise it could happen again! ...

Sarah I'll make a deal with you. You find out why we nearly blew it. OK, you research it, you analyse it, and then when you blow it again, you can phone me up and explain it to me.

Joe (*laughing*) It's a deal. Anyway, so listen, what happened about the pains, it obviously wasn't a relapse so how are you, what was it?

Sarah No, it's not a relapse and don't panic, but I do have to have an operation ...

The stuffing goes out of Joe

Joe Oh ...

Sarah Yes. I saw the specialist again after I spoke to you and he was sure it *was* the neuropathy, but I wanted a second opinion and this new man is certain from the pattern of the discomfort that it's not and there's an infection, so he's going to operate ...

Joe is shocked, but stays controlled so as not to heap his fear onto her

Joe I see. I see ...

Sarah I didn't want my first call back to mention this because I knew you'd be upset and because it means putting back flying over to see you, but it's irresponsible not to tell, isn't it?

Joe Oh yes, oh no you did right, if you have to have it, yes ... (*His mind jumps away from the fear to something less painful*) So you did your play with this pain and through all these medical examinations, did you?

Sarah I didn't have any choice.

Joe God, you've got more balls than Sherpa Tensing ...

Sarah Who's Sherpa Tensing?

Joe He was the first man to climb ... I mean you've got a lot of guts ...

She goes a little quieter

Sarah Not really. I'm pretty scared actually, remembering the last couple of times I was in ...

Joe (*very quietly*) Oh shit, Sarah ...

She injects some casualness

Sarah Yeah, well, you know, all that cutting and thrusting, it's like something out of *The Three Musketeers* ... (*Laughing*) I guess that's why I felt like talking to someone literary about it ...

But he speaks to her fears and his

Joe (*quietly*) Oh Sarah, you'll be all right, I know you will; I'll pray for you, I'll pray for you, I will.

She interrupts, laughing and very lively

Sarah Thank you Joe, but I'm not sure my God listens to you Goyim, so I think you're wasting your time.

Joe manages to hold back an eruption of laughter to speak his next line

Joe Well, taking all the circumstances into account, it's the best I can manage! ...

... and now erupts into glorious, whole-hearted laughter, slapping his leg, rocking. Sarah shouts through it

Sarah (*laughing, happy*) Green! I am going into the hospital for an operation, why are you laughing, Green!? ...

But he can't stop, as the full sense of the absurd side of their situation hits him

Green! ... You are an agoraphobic depressive with complications, this hilarity doesn't fit your patterns, Green! ...

His laughter gradually subsides

Joe Oh Sarah ... oh my God ... listen, I'm not laughing at your operation, darling, I'm laughing at us, I'm laughing at me.
Sarah OK, so tell me something funny about yourself, we need it, believe me ...

He has recovered and adjusts himself

Joe Something funny? Well it's not funny exactly, but anyway something positive, OK, remember when I said just now I had something important to tell you? ...
Sarah When I phoned and you did your "I am being very humble" act, I remember, yes.
Joe Maybe, but I didn't abandon you either, I've got an idea for a play and I'm ready to start working ...

She doesn't immediately grasp any further implication in this announcement

Sarah (*excited for him*) Joe, that's terrific, what happened, how come?! ...
Joe (*suddenly mumbling*) Well, well, I ... wel ...
Sarah (*calling*) Can't hear you any more!
Joe (*more firmly but still hesitantly*) Sorry, well I, I, well when I couldn't phone you, when I couldn't well communicate with you at all I ... well I started to think of writing, I don't know, it just, well it just started to come back.
Sarah But that's wonderful, you're starting, that's wonderful! ...
Joe And of course there'd be a leading part for you.
Sarah (*with mock arrogance*) I should think so ...
Joe Ah, yes. But there's a catch. There's a little problem, see.

Her irony returns

Sarah Surprise me, Joe ...
Joe See, I need you to help me with it ...

Now the full meaning dawns on her. A beat

Sarah Ahh ...

Joe goes blithely on

Joe Oh, I don't mean with the actual lines, but I mean with the preparation, talking through the structure, the actual plot, I can't, I can't, well ...
Sarah Of course.
Joe ... See the plot's based on my childhood in America, when I was sent away, the family over there, and so on, but I go to the typewriter and it's too ... I ... (*Quieter*) Well it's too lonely ...
Sarah But of course, what else ...

He defends himself against her tone

Joe Look, what's all this, "Ah, ah, but of course, but of course," you don't sound very pleased, I must say.
Sarah While I was working on the Tennessee Williams, I used to wonder what way you'd find to try and get your grabby little claws into me, of course I missed the obvious one ...
Joe (*defending himself*) Listen, can we forget my convoluted motives at this point, if this works out I get a play and you get a part, partner, let's concentrate on that for a minute, can we, hmm?
Sarah (*quietly serious*) Joe. I never met anybody who needed me like you do. But if you try and nail me to the wall like a trophy I'll hobble out of your life for good this time. I mean it ...
Joe (*down*) I understand ...
Sarah Yes, but I don't just mean understand in words, not "I understand Sarah, I understand", but in the bone, in the marrow, do you understand me, in the marrow, Joe, I mean it. I'll go.

Joe hesitates a fraction ...

Joe I under ... (*Quietly*) ... yes ...
Sarah OK. I'll come and help you with your play. I was coming anyway, dolt, so I'll come.

Joe is over the moon

Joe Wonderful, when, when can we start!?
Sarah The operation's on the fourteenth and I get out on the seventeenth, give me ten days to get over it, pack, I'll be with you on the twenty-eighth.
Joe Wonderful. (*Suddenly quieter*) Sarah, why did you phone back?
Sarah For a five year, five-times-a-week-on-the-couch-man, you don't understand much, do you, teach? See you on the twenty-eighth. I have to go now.

He speaks swiftly to hold her

Joe Sarah! ...
Sarah What?
Joe (*humbly*) I'm sorry about San Francisco. You were right, I'm sorry ...
Sarah I'm watching you, Joe, I've got my eyes on your grabby little claws *all* the time ...
Joe And Sarah ...

Sarah I have to use the phone, I have to talk to the specialist.

Joe can't immediately say the final thing that is on his mind. After a beat, Sarah is exasperated by the silence on the other end of the phone

   Joe! . . .

Her tone drives him to speak

Joe (*muttering*) Don't die, Sarah . . .
Sarah (*making light of it*) But it'll make a wonderful first act curtain!
Joe (*muttering; down*) I don't like those kinds of play . . .
Sarah (*gently*) See you on the twenty-eighth, I'll speak to you, bye . . .

He can't reply. She waits, then puts the phone down gently and waits a moment. He gets straight up and crosses to the vacuum cleaner. She picks up the phone and dials

Sarah Hello, can I speak to Dr Saltzman please? . . . OK, I'll hold . . .

Joe suddenly does a series of mock karate moves and chops, accompanied by made-up Japanese attacking words

Joe Hazzamaku! . . . Kamakazechomazi! . . . Hakamakamuuuu! . . .

Joe is winning

Sarah holds on the phone

The Lights fade to Black-Out

SCENE 2

Three weeks later

It is around 10 a.m. in London, 5 a.m. in New York

   Sarah's room is dark and empty, the bed clothes folded back for airing. Joe's room, empty at lights up, is very neat. Anything like the odd paper, pullover, etc., is cleared away. There is a large bunch of flowers in a vase for the first time and the room looks as good as the permanent items will allow. We hear Joe's voice off-stage, coming from the outside door direction

Joe (*off*) That's it . . . it's through there, go right through, will you?

A pause until Sarah enters on crutches followed by Joe, who reaches past her to hold the room door wide open

Sarah waits a moment. She wears a neat, expensive suit under her coat and carries a large handbag. Joe is in "slim" clothes for the first time and looks his best so far. He is over solicitous about her condition and nervous throughout the scene, though very happy to see her at the same time. She is a little nervous too, but far more relaxed than him

Joe Shall I take your coat or would you rather? . . .

Sarah Oh, thank you . . .

She takes off her coat, the logistics of which she is used to with crutches and large handbag, but which is intricate. Joe, who has never seen her in action before, moves to help at one point

Joe Shall I? . . .
Sarah It's OK, thank you . . . (*Taking her normal time, she finally hands him the coat, retaining her handbag*) Thank you.
Joe Right. I'll just hang this up . . .

He takes the coat out into the corridor to hang it up, but re-appears immediately

Oh, do sit down, sit down please, wherever you like . . .
Sarah Thanks . . . (*She sits in one of the armchairs*)

Joe hangs up the coat outside and returns

Joe (*seeing where she's sitting down*) Ah fine, right, is that chair all right, it's OK, is it? Or would you rather sit on the sofa or is it too low, it's too low, is it? . . .
Sarah (*soothing his nervous concern with her voice*) This one's fine, I like it, it's very comfortable.
Joe Oh good, right, tea, coffee, orange juice, I've got fresh orange juice, well fresh in a carton, you know, do you like that or tea or coffee . . . (*Suddenly remembering*) Or chocolate, I've got hot chocolate. So that's tea, coffee, orange juice, hot chocolate, what would you like?
Sarah Just some hot water, if that's all right, thank you.
Joe (*taken aback*) Hot water? . . .
Sarah Yes please.
Joe Erm is that, do you want, I mean boiled water right, I mean you don't just want it hot straight from the . . . no, of course, boiled of course—with sugar, do you take sugar with it? . . .
Sarah (*calming him*) Joe. Everything's fine, the operation was fine, I feel fine, I'm not going to fall apart. I flew across the Atlantic yesterday, I'm OK, just a cup of plain, boiled water.
Joe (*hanging his head a little*) I'm sorry, I'm a gibbering wreck, God I imagined myself being so relaxed when you came. (*He tries to shake off his nerves by making a joke of his condition, addressing the room*) I am a man, I am a grown up, middle aged man, I am not a child. I have been married, I have signed contracts, I drive a car, I know how to change gear, this proves I am grown up; I have a cheque book, I wear long trousers, I know how a vagina works and I will now go and get you some boiled water . . .

She laughs a lot as he exits with big, "grown up" strides . . . only to reappear almost immediately at the door

Joe No sugar, right? . . .
Sarah (*laughing*) Yes!! . . .

Joe disappears once more

She looks around the room and adjusts her hair a little

  Joe reappears, Mr Efficient

Joe Kettle's just boiling, electric, right ... (*He lights a cigarette. He recaptures some poise*)

Joe So ... How are you, how's the hotel, are you jet-lagged?

Sarah I don't think so, I slept most of yesterday at the hotel, so I feel pretty good.

Joe And the hotel's OK, is it?

Sarah It's very nice, you found me a nice place.

Joe Oh good ...

Sarah They're very pleasant, people step back for me at the doors and elevators, they don't do that much at home. My God, Joe, you really are slim, aren't you?

He jumps up and gets a photo down from a shelf and takes it to her

Joe Here. Look at this. This is me outside the theatre in the West End at the first night of *The Empty Palate*, I was on tranquillisers then, so I could still travel ...

She studies the picture

Sarah My God ... I wouldn't have recognised you.

Joe I know. Nineteen stone, that was my peak.

Sarah (*handing the photo back*) That's incredible, you've done marvels.

Joe (*putting the photo back on the shelf*) Good, isn't it? ... (*He sits*)

A beat as Sarah looks round

Sarah This room's very pleasant, this is where I talk to you, right?

Joe Yes, that's right, it's the irregular shape I think, and the steps going up out of it, gives it a bit of character, doesn't it?

Sarah Really nice, I feel comfortable in it.

Joe Oh good ... (*A beat ... he starts*) Oh, plain boiled water coming up, the kettle ...

  Joe exits

Sarah waits, at ease

  Joe is suddenly back

  Anything with it, toast, a boiled egg, poached egg, scrambled, anything at all?

Sarah No thanks, I had breakfast at the hotel.

  Joe's away again and returns after a moment with a mug of boiled water

Joe gets a chair, puts it next to her and puts the mug onto it—he has no spare side table

Joe There you are, is that all right?

Sarah Thank you. (*She sips the water*)

Joe watches. A beat

Joe Is it all right?
Sarah Yes, it's . . .
Joe (*interrupting*) Is that how you have it? . . .
Sarah (*firmly but kindly*) Joe. This is without any doubt the finest boiled water I ever drank anywhere in the world.
Joe (*shrugging*) Shit, I think I'll go and breathe into a paper bag, or something . . .

She chuckles through her drink. He sits. A beat. They look at each other for the first time . . .

So the flight was all right, was it? . . .
Sarah We've been over the flight and the hotel, we did that bit.
Joe True . . . (*He rises and goes and shakes her hand*) Right then, I think that covers everything, it's been really nice meeting you, goodbye . . .

She smiles up at him, he turns and goes back to the chair

I know how a vagina works, I wear long trousers, I shave . . . (*He sits and crosses his legs*)

A longer pause as they look at each other

Sarah How do I look, Joe?

His nervousness contradictorily makes him speak what he actually thinks first

Joe (*low*) You're beautiful . . . I mean you look very nice . . .
Sarah Thank you, stick with the beautiful, I like it.

A beat. Joe's tension shows itself in that he leans heavily on one arm of the chair

Do the crutches bother you, I mean the slow walk and all?
Joe Not at all, not in the slightest.
Sarah You can say, Joe, let's not start that way.

He looks straight at her to prove he means it

Joe It doesn't bother me at all, at *all* . . .

She smiles. A beat. He looks down

How about me?
Sarah You're not as good-looking as your voice, but you're very attractive.
Joe Oh . . .
Sarah I'm not disappointed, really.
Joe How do you mean my voice sounds good-looking?
Sarah Your voice on the phone sounds like Richard Burton.
Joe Oh . . . Richard Burton had very bad spots, you know . . .

She laughs

Sarah Joe, I'm not disappointed.

Joe (*shocked*) Oh . . . Thank you . . . (*A long pause, he looks down*) Nor am I . . .

Pause. Joe is very tense, Sarah is not

Sarah How do you want to play this?
Joe (*not understanding exactly*) Sorry? . . .
Sarah Shall we go to bed now?
Joe (*astonished and afraid*) What! . . .
Sarah Well, you said you weren't disappointed . . .

Joe's mind is confusion

Joe No, I'm not. I . . .
Sarah (*smiling*) You mean you think we should date some more first? . . .
Joe No . . . I—
Sarah (*going on*) I kind of thought we'd dated enough on the phone.

Joe can hardly speak

Joe Erm, er . . . Yes. (*He clears his throat and stops*)

Sarah suddenly realises that she has mistaken the situation. She is genuinely ashamed and embarrassed

Sarah (*quietly*) Joe, I'm terribly sorry . . . When you said you weren't disappointed either, I . . . I mean I think I mistook your signal there completely, I'm really sorry . . .
Joe (*mumbling*) 'S all right . . .
Sarah At home in this type of . . . I mean, those words . . . I'm terribly sorry . . .

Her retreat brings him forward a little

Joe (*quietly, with the beginnings of a joke*) A bit grabby on your part there I think . . .
Sarah (*laughing out loud*) Maybe you're right there, maestro, maybe you are at that! . . .

Pause as they recompose themselves. Joe is looking down, though

Joe (*quietly*) I'm really glad you're here at last, though.
Sarah Thank you.

A longer pause

Joe Why do you drink hot water?
Sarah Well. I used to think it was part of the general health kick that's around, but it started after my relapse, so I guess it's some kind of trying to clean my body out.
Joe Ah, yes.

Pause

(*A bit down*) I never asked you properly how *Small Craft Warnings* went, either. I'm really sorry about that . . .

Sarah suddenly realises something

Sarah (*interrupting*) Oh look, let's work, let's work, OK, this is crazy. We scream at each other down the phone and now we're sitting here like a North Korean and an Eskimo on a blind date in the Hilton, it's crazy, it's schizophrenic, let's just work for a couple of days and then, you know, I mean this is horrible . . .

Joe rises

Joe The girl is right. You're absolutely right, we'll work and then in discussion and in between the cups of boiled water and then . . . exactly, right. (*He's pacing*) Well I've got a story, the characters, but I haven't got the through line, how the story works itself out, in other words I've got Hamlet having to kill his father.

Sarah (*interrupting*) Having to kill his uncle, you mean.

Joe doesn't care about the slip

Joe Kill his uncle, that's right, but the journey, how the thing unfolds, that's what I don't have.

Sarah OK, well let's hear what you do have.

Joe Right ! Notes! . . . (*He marches to the white table with the typewriter on it and sits and picks up some papers. In doing so, he becomes aware of the machine in front of him. He puts the sheets aside and stares at the machine. Quietly*) God . . .

Sarah Nice, huh, long-time-no-touch . . .

Joe does indeed touch the machine more

Joe Wonderful . . . (*He turns the motor on and off a few times, then turns it off and looks at Sarah, moved by the fact he's going to write with her help. Quietly*) Sarah. Before I knew the operation was all right . . . when I didn't know if you'd, before I heard from you, I . . . (*He stops. A big feeling is coming*)

Sarah (*quietly*) Joe . . .

Her voice makes him speak to stop her

Joe (*emphatically*) When I thought I might not see you . . .

He stops again. She remains silent. He speaks deliberately to make sure it comes out right this time, but still quiet

I might never see you, I . . . (*He suddenly puts a hand over his eyes to stop the emerging tears*)

Pause

Sarah (*quietly*) Thank you.

Suddenly he rips the tears away from his eyes and changes gear completely. He is up, pacing, firm, enthusiastic

Joe Right. Enough of that, right, the story so far . . . (*He looks at the notes in his hand, shuffles the pages to bring the top page to the top, and so on, and*

*as he does so his mind changes direction to offering Sarah some explanation.
Quieter)* ... You see, I have such rage towards my parents, buried still,
still buried, that's why it's difficult to ... to, you know, make it coherent
as a play, you see.
Sarah That's OK.

Again Joe brushes feelings aside in the interests of the work in hand

Joe Right. Excellent, here we go, we're in New York, World War Two, an
American family, the father a salesman—OK, father, mother, two
daughters, foster son, yours truly, OK. What I don't know is the
relationships, is he accepted by the mother in particular, how does it all
work out, that's what I can't get right, really ...

The Lights fade to Black-Out

SCENE 3

That night

It is 3 a.m. in London, 10 p.m. in New York

*Both rooms are in darkness, save for such moonlight or street lighting which
may creep in through windows*

*Joe enters in vest and pants. He goes to the standard lamp and turns it on—
there is gentle light. He picks up a cigarette from the coffee table and lights it,
stands a moment, then goes to the round, plastic table and picks up the notes he
and Sarah had been working on for the play, shakes them into a neater though
thin pile, picks up a pencil and walks to the sofa*

*He sits down on the sofa and starts to look through the notes ... He underlines
something, he crosses something else out and writes another word. He goes on
reading. He now looks at one page for quite a long time ... And he begins to
cry. He sits there crying for a little and quite quickly the crying comes from a
very deep place in him, from the deepest place. And he sits there, notes about a
play about his childhood in New York in his hand and weeps the bitterest,
deepest most enormous tears, in gulps and sobs and moans. And it is as if the
feelings that are coming out are bigger than his body could contain. And in a
way they are, for he is weeping the Atlantic Ocean that he crossed away from
his mother in tears. And he is weeping for the loss of her beauty and comfort
and utter loveliness. And he is weeping for the loss of the family he lost, his two
sisters and his other mother and father when he had to return. And he weeps
utterly for his lost life and loves, for he was cast out like an angel into hell, and
he is feeling that he is utterly alone in the universe and without love, as he felt
all that lifetime ago. And he weeps. And once or twice it may seem that he is
stopping, but the loss only returns more deeply, that separation from beauty
and safety to terror and guilt and the sobbing resumes with strange sounds of
"Burrrr" and "Errr" a moaning chant to comfort himself. And somewhere in
all of this he apologises aloud for the crime which children who are thrown out
for ever think they must have committed ...*

Joe I'm sorry ... I'm sorry ...

And he gets up weeping and walks around the room in the "now" but still weeping the past, and goes back and sits, gulping

And eventually, and it seems like a lifetime, and it is, he slowly stops sobbing and returns to "now". And there is the odd sob and it is over. And he sits, breathing some deep breaths. And he wipes his face free of tears. And sits a little longer ...

Then he goes to the phone and dials three numbers. It answers. His voice is quite thick, but he speaks quite calmly

Oh yes, hello, could I have an alarm call for eight-thirty please ... That's right ... three-seven-nine four-nine-zero-two ... Thank you very much, goodnight. (*And he puts down the phone, goes to the standard lamp and turns it off*)

The Lights fade to Black-Out

SCENE 4

Next day

Immediately Joe exits from Scene Three we hear Sarah's voice in the dark

Sarah's Voice Joe, I've just finished my supper here at the hotel—salad and plenty of boiled water, ho, ho, ho—and I just wanted to say a couple of things to you on tape before I go to bed. I'm not usually afraid to speak out, as you know, but I thought you might not want to hear this face-to-face right now. Well first, it's been terrific working with you. Of course I'm not telling you how to do your job, but honestly you don't need to stay up nights checking over the notes and making yourself tired for the daytime; I promise you, I can tell from just these two days it's going to be a wonderful play. Also, Joe—and this is why I'm making this little broadcast, really—forgetting the bungling way I introduced it when I arrived, I do want to make love to you very much. I hope my handicap won't mean we have to make love in ways that aren't exciting for you, but if you want to go ahead I'm sure we can work things out, but of course it's completely up to you. I'm going to leave this tape with you tomorrow after we finish and if you want to talk to me on the phone about it, that's fine, or not if you don't, no pressure. Good night, Joe, I'll see you in the morning. Good night now ...

It is important to note that the above speech comes on the day between scenes 3 and 5

SCENE 5

Next day

The Lights come up in Joe's room

Joe is tidying up. The bell goes. He takes a deep breath and goes out

After a moment Sarah enters in a different outfit from two days ago. Joe has taken off and hung up her coat outside. She sits in the same chair she did in the

previous scene, putting her crutches and handbag beside it. Joe follows her in;
he's very tense

Joe Right . . . Good, did you sleep all right, how are you?
Sarah I'm sleeping really well, how about you, you weren't up all last night
being creative again, were you?
Joe No, I slept quite well, would you like something to drink?
Sarah No thanks.
Joe Right . . .
Sarah Hey, what're you so grouchy about, don't you like what we worked
on yesterday?
Joe Oh no, no I think it's fine, I think it's going extremely well . . .

He lights a cigarette. She ignores his mood for the moment

Sarah Did you get a chance to look over it last night?
Joe Yes, yes I did, no, no, it's fine, it's all right.
Sarah Well we got to the point of one of the daughters' jealousy, didn't we,
so should we start there, 'cos I think the lead into that works, don't you?

Joe paces

Joe Yes. Yes that all works very well . . .
Sarah You don't sound convinced. Do you want to go back over the notes
from the start and see if we've missed anything?
Joe (*down*) No, I don't think there's any need for that.
Sarah (*cheerfully*) Joe, you're being obtuse, I think your genius is deserting
you and you need a bit of straight New York know-how. OK, simple
question, do you want to start from where we got to or go back and lead
into it?
Joe (*quite down*) It doesn't matter, wherever you like, yes where we stopped
is fine, wherever you like . . .

She now fully senses something is wrong, but carries on for the moment after a
beat to let him say something, which he doesn't . . .

Sarah (*quieter*) So we'll start from that point, OK.

Joe is pacing or standing somewhere, ill-at-ease

Joe Yes . . .

She sees he's really tense, but allows it. After a beat, he has to fill the silence

Yes, that's right, from er, from that point . . .

A beat

Sarah (*soothing*) Do you want a break today, shall we just talk or do
nothing? This is all new to you, writing again, isn't it?
Joe No, it's not . . . it's er . . . no . . .
Sarah (*heartily; concealing worry*) Come on, we can take a break for a day
for Christ's sake, let's do that, let's just talk and relax, OK?

Finally . . .

Joe (*tense, grim*) Sarah. I can't write the play. I can't write it . . .

She doesn't speak, waiting to understand

> We've got to stop. I won't be able to write the play. I feel incredibly tense, my head's full of concrete. We have to stop, it's been like this since you came . . .

A beat

Sarah (*quietly*) OK.
Joe I mean I just can't, I can't, that's it, I can't . . .
Sarah That's OK. . . .
Joe (*grim but not loud*) Oh, stop being so bloody understanding, it's not OK! This is the unresolved mess called me. I throw out the only thing I love who came three thousand miles to see me, that's how it is . . .

She tries to rescue them after a beat

Sarah (*quietly*) Well, if you love me, why throw me out?

He gestures with head and arms to mean everything's impossible

> (*Quietly*) D'you want me to stay and just talk, we could just talk and have some tea or whatever?

Joe (*down*) No. You have to go. There's no point . . .

Pause. He can't say anything. She tries one more time

Sarah (*quietly*) I mean we don't have to work or anything . . .
Joe (*muttering*) 'S impossible . . .

She sees that it is for him

Sarah (*quietly*) It's all right. You're just not ready yet. You thought you were, but you're not, that's all . . .
Joe That's right. I'm not ready . . .

Pause. There's no way through for her. She is deeply hurt but valiant

Sarah Don't feel bad. If you can't, you can't . . .

He is again pacing, talking bitterly, more to himself

Joe What a joke, what a farce, eh, wonderful; all the time you were on the way, from the moment you said you were coming, I had these ridiculous fantasies, I played out these ridiculous scenes in my mind of me taking you off to bed and us making glorious love and living happily ever after and all that guff, and then you'd act in my play and now look what it *really* is . . . (*Angrily at her*) I told you, didn't I, I warned you, I told you on the phone! . . .

She in turn has looked down. Pause

Sarah (*low*) You'll write when you're ready . . .

Joe (*turning on her and shouting*) We're not talking about writing, we're talking about me throwing you out and away for ever!! ...

She puts her hand to her face and eyes to cover the tears that are unstoppable this time

Sarah Oh Joe ...

Pause as he paces. Then he delivers the final cruelty from his hurt

Joe (*not loud*) And I sold the statue.
Sarah (*talking through her feelings*) Excuse me, you, I don't ...
Joe I sold the statue of Joe Louis, I sold the statue you gave me.

Silence. She waits, hurting

    (*Down and grim*) It wasn't perfect, so I sold it. It was a nice statue, but it wasn't beautiful ...

What can she say or do? A beat

    (*Quietly*) I sold it for eighty pounds ...

A beat

Sarah (*hopelessly*) Well, it was a gift, it was yours, so you can do what you want with it ...
Joe (*roaring*) I'm saying I disposed of the statue! ...

There is a long pause. Joe leans against something, looking down. Sarah looks out of the window

Sarah (*quietly but clearly*) You want to chop me up into little pieces, don't you? ...

He can't speak. A beat

    And then you want to put all the pieces together again and torture me with electric shocks and hear me scream and then boil me in oil and jump on the bits, don't you? ...

He puts his hands up to his face ... and nods ... A pause

    (*Quietly*) I wanted to do that to all of them when I first got ill and they hurt me and wouldn't help me ...

A beat. She's still looking out of the window

    And you love me ...

She doesn't need to see him nod despairingly behind her. She sighs

    I'll call a cab.

He points to a phone book

She gets up and goes without her crutches slowly to the book, finds the number, goes to the phone and dials

(*on the phone*) Yes, I'd like a taxi now at eighty-six Farely Road, please . . .
to go to Belsize Park . . . three-seven-nine four-nine-zero-two . . . thank
you . . . (*She replaces the receiver*) Ten minutes. (*She goes back to her
chair*)

*He stands there for a moment. He'd like to cry but can't; she'd like to cry but
won't. Long pause . . . suddenly he has to do something to fill the ten minutes*

Joe (*muttering*) I'll get your coat . . .

He exits, fetches her coat and returns

*She gets up, waiting for it. He hands it to her and goes to sit, head down. She
sits, having put on the coat. Pause. She reaches into her bag and takes out the
cassette tape in its case*

Sarah I've got a tape for you.
Joe What is it?
Sarah Just a couple of things I wanted to say. Maybe you'll listen to it when
you're feeling better . . .
Joe (*muttering*) Just put it somewhere . . .

She puts the cassette down. Silence

Is your air ticket valid for today? You won't have to buy another ticket on
top of everything else, will you?
Sarah No, it's valid, don't worry.

Pause . . . suddenly he can't bear it. He tears himself up

Joe (*muttering*) I'm going into the bedroom . . . (*He starts to go*)
Sarah (*quietly*) I love you, Joe.

He whips round to her and roars

Joe DON'T SAY THAT TO ME! DON'T SAY THAT THING TO ME!

Sarah jumps from the force of his despairing feelings

   Joe rushes out

She sits . . . She clears her throat once. She waits

The Lights fade to Black-Out

SCENE 6

One week later. Sunday

It is 5.30 p.m. in London, 12.30 p.m. in New York

*Sarah, dressed in her dressing gown, dials Joe's number. It rings in Joe's empty
room*

After a time Joe enters, annoyed, and goes to the phone, talking at it

Joe What, what, Im busy, what!? . . . (*He picks up the phone; sharply*)
  Yes! . . .
Sarah Hello, it's me.

*He puts the receiver away from his ear in an instinctive rejection, then puts it
down carefully on the sofa, and moves away from it, half looking at it. He sits
in an armchair, looking at the phone. A beat*

  Hello? . . . (*She waits*) . . . Hello? . . . (*She waits*) . . . Joe?

Pause

  Joe, can you hear me? . . .

Pause

  (*Shouting*) I'm just calling to say hello, I'm only calling to say hello . . .

*He hears a slight sound, creeps to the phone and puts a cushion over it ever so
carefully*

  Joe creeps out of the room

Sarah waits . . .

  Joe? . . . (*She waits. Shouting*) I know you're there because the line's still
  open! . . . (*A beat*) I'm just calling to say hello! . . .

Pause

  Joe? . . . (*Finally she gives up and in a rage slams the phone down*) Jesus
  Christ, who invented happiness anyway?!! (*A beat*)

The Lights fade to Black-Out

SCENE 7

Four months later

It is 1 p.m. in London, 8 a.m. in New York

Sarah is asleep in bed

*Joe enters from the kitchen carrying a bowl full of tinned peaches. He is at one
and the same time very nervous about phoning Sarah, because of the
importance of the call and how he treated her when he saw her, and very happy
because he feels he can now treat her better. When he first speaks to her, he
disguises any worries or guilt he may feel with extreme perkiness; in fact he's
"high". He sits on the sofa, eats some peaches for comfort, takes a few
breaths, looks at some bills, looks at his watch, and, nervous, dials the number*

  *The phone rings in Sarah's room. She wakes after a moment and sleepily
  answers it, struggling to awake*

Sarah Hello? . . .

Joe (*very perky*) Good morning, Ms, this is your early morning alarm call, at the third stroke it will be eight a.m. New York time . . .

Sarah (*still waking and not enthusiastic*) Hello Joe . . .

Joe . . . I did not, of course, know whether you'd be in, but remembering that eight was the approximate time at which you rose to earn a crust, I took the liberty of ringing.

Sarah (*sarcastically*) I'm glad you're so cheerful, Joe.

Joe (*oblivious*) And why shouldn't I be, I am a man in tune with himself and I am eating a family-sized tin of peaches from an oven-proof glass bowl.

Sarah sits and stretches

Sarah Back to your old ways, huh?

Joe Sarah, life is very complicated; the mind is complicated, the world is complicated, as a matter of fact everything is pretty complicated, actually . . .

Sarah (*yawning*) For a pain-in-the-ass who hasn't phoned for four months you sure come out with some very profound thoughts before breakfast, friend . . .

Joe (*pretending to be completely unperturbed*) This is true, this is very true, but even a person of the genus you describe, the pain-in-the-*arts* genus, even such low-lifes may, paradoxically, utter profound truths, thus they may go back to eating their peaches while at the same time developing in new directions, this is the essence of our contradictory world . . .

Sarah I'm going for a pee . . .

She gets out of bed and leaves the room on crutches

Left 'alone', Joe is again apprehensive about how this will come out

Joe (*to himself*) Some people cannot grasp profound ideas at eight in the morning without first going to the toilet . . . (*He delves deep into the peaches, then picks up a bill from the ones he had glanced at earlier. He sees something worrying suddenly . . . It's a final demand for a large phone bill to be paid!*) What! God! (*He fumbles around on the table for a pen and cheque-book, phone still in the other hand*)

Sarah's alarm utters its electric "bips". Joe starts a little, as he hears the alarm, thinking it is Sarah returning

Your alarm's going off!

Sarah returns, refreshed. She switches off the alarm, and picks up the phone

Sarah I *am* going to work, so I don't have long, this had better be good . . .

Joe (*again perky*) Hello again, Ms Wise, and may I say straight away that I do not apologise for my behaviour during your visit, apology implies guilt and I am not guilty, I have a sickness, one, I hasten to add, which is becoming less sick with every passing day.

Sarah (*flatly*) I called you half a dozen times, the first time you wouldn't speak to me, the others you put the phone down, I don't know what's less sick about that . . .

Joe What is less sick is that having indeed put the phone *down*, I have now picked it *up*, any trained person in the field would *immediately* grasp the significance of this . . .

Sarah A trained person in the field would immediately grasp that you're full of what's lying all *over* the field which is horse-shit, friend, believe me . . .

Joe I see I have not yet convinced you of the profound changes I am undergoing, I pass therefore to minor matters, your illness, how is the illness, where is the illness, *is* the illness? . . .

Sarah (*flatly*) Yes, I still have relapsive peripheral polyneuropathy of unknown origin.

It hits Joe that his "high" has gone too far this time. A beat

Joe (*low*) Sorry . . .

Sarah (*annoyed*) Listen, crud, what d'ya mean you won't apologise for kicking me out and selling my statue *and* putting the phone down, what the hell kind of a per . . .

Joe (*interrupting; cheery again with fake defiance*) I knew it, here we go, recriminations . . .

Sarah Recriminations! I'm just asking for a sign that you recognise that you . . .

Joe (*interrupting again*) Of course, recriminations, *your* illness is an illness, *my* illness is being a rat, that's the way they slice it, the world is full of priests, you are Moses with the tablets, I am a bad person, thus ignorance is satisfied . . .

Sarah gets out of bed and goes to brush her hair and get ready for work at the dressing-table, taking the phone with her

Sarah Joe, my boss doesn't set the working hours of his employees to annoy *you*, we call that paranoia, sweetheart, I actually have, in the real world, to clock in on time at Langland, Boyer, Bergson and Smallwood, attorneys-at-law, I really do . . . (*She brushes her hair with some difficulty, as she still has the phone to her ear*)

Joe I see. So you do not wish to know the reason for my call?

Sarah No.

Joe I see. So you do not wish to know what is lying at this very moment on the round, plastic-topped table behind me?

Sarah You're a crud, Green . . .

Joe Well, whether . . .

Sarah (*going straight on*) . . . and I'm a crud for talking to a crud.

Joe Sticks and stones may break my bones, very well, on the round, plastic-topped table behind me lie seventy-three pages of a corrected second draft of an as yet untitled play. It is a play full of joy and pain, of passion and despair, in a word, it is a masterpiece. It will elevate me from the level of a slightly known, third rank writer to the level of a slightly *better* known third rank writer . . . (*His tone changes*) . . . and the dedication on the first page is to you . . .

Sarah I didn't come over for a play, Joe. I came over for you.

Joe (*low*) I know . . .

Sarah (*suddenly shouting*) Then apologise, God-damn you!

All the "high" is knocked out of Joe

Joe (*quietly*) I'm sorry. I apologise . . .

Sarah (*still angry*) Jesus! . . . (*Angry still*) OK . . . (*And still pretty angry*) I'm
glad for your sake you got a play out.

Joe now tries to be kind

Joe (*quietly*) It's the same one, the one we started about my childhood in
America, I managed it alone . . .

Sarah (*flatly*) Congratulations.

Joe (*quietly; humbly*) I'd like you to perform it . . .

Sarah (*hard*) Fine, send it, is it any good, has it been produced yet?

Joe (*low*) No. It's for you . . .

Sarah Fine. Send it, I'll have a look at it.

Pause. Sarah goes on with her preparations, as if only they were occupying her

Joe (*low*) I think it's come out pretty well . . .

Sarah Joe, I can't get ready with one hand, send the play.

Joe has to ask the dangerous question or the phone will go down

Joe (*low*) Sarah. What's going to happen?

Sarah I'm going to Bergson and Smallwood and you're going to send me
the play. Bergson likes cripples.

Joe No, I mean what's going to *happen*?

*She goes on in her matter-of-fact way and tone preparing to leave, though she
knows what's coming*

Sarah I'm going to work, you send me the play, I'll read it and if I like it and
you don't want to change anything, then you'll try and set it up here,
that's what's going to happen.

Joe goes for it

Joe (*quieter*) Sarah, come and live with me . . .

She slams down her brush so hard it flies off somewhere. She is outraged

Sarah I knew it! I knew it! I knew from the moment I heard that creepy,
grabby, manic everything-is-happy-and-forgotten-darling tone in your
voice, I knew, I knew, you're crazy, you know that, I told you you weren't
crazy, but you're crazy, you have a genuine screw loose, correction, you
have the whole Steel Corporation of America loose! . . . live with you, I
was living with you, well over there, and you *threw me out*! You threw me
out at *ten minutes notice and* my statue. Jesus! . . .

*She pauses for breath. Joe is quiet and rational. He's thought about all of it for
a long time. He has prepared serious answers*

Joe Sarah, I genuinely believe . . .

Sarah (*interrupting*) ... and I'd just told you I wanted to sleep with you, we were going to work on the play and bingo, out, goodbye! Ladybird, ladybird, screw off and now you want ... Jesus, Moses and Joseph, this guy is a true original, Joe you're living on the fourth storey of a two storey building, believe me, you are, you are! ... (*She pauses for breath*)

Joe (*quietly*) I genuinely believe I have good cause to know that it will not occur again, it cannot hap ...

Sarah (*interrupting; still in justified overdrive*) Oh, you believe, you have good cause and so I'm just supposed ... (*A touch slower and quieter*) Joe, I really wanted to help, I did, and I thought there was a home for me in that maelstrom inside you, but I was wrong, you've got a volcano in there, Joe, I mean you're really blazing and I can't help that, I like volcanos, but I don't want to screw one, I don't want to jump into one, believe me, I'm sick but I'm no masochist, really, forget it, really ...

Joe (*quietly; calmly*) But you said you loved me ...

Sarah And I do, I do love you, I love a volcano, so? I have problems, I need my head examining, as well as my nervous system, terrific.

Joe (*quietly*) I love you too.

Sarah Wonderful, tremendous, I love a volcano and the volcano loves me back, so? (*She goes quieter for the first time*) Joe. Joey, please understand, please try to understand, I don't trust it, I don't trust you, Joe, how can I, I can't risk that again, Joe, and I won't, try to see what I see, please, it was a nightmare for me, it was, Joe, it was ... (*Pause. Roaring*) You hurt me!

Joe (*quiet and calm still*) I don't believe there will be any need for this and I only offer it as a kind of reassurance, but I could purchase a second-hand caravan and park it outside my flat and then you could always go to the ...

Whether she has been standing or sitting, Sarah collapses in total, helpless laughter, she literally falls down wherever she is. Joe tries an occasional "I ... I ...", but has to allow the worst to pass. Finally

I'm not actually saying we get one, I only meant it as ...

She roars away. He waits

I'm not saying that ...

She finally gets herself mentally, physically, and vocally together a bit

Sarah A caravan, a caravan, right, that's it? ...

Joe It's only an attempt to give you some ...

Sarah (*interrupting*) No, no, I understand, we're living together, we eat, we make love, we work on the play, suddenly rumble, rumble, rumble, the volcano, me hobble, hobble, hobble to the caravan to safety. While the eruption is at its height, we wave to each other through the window, I catch my crutches on the primus stove, the eruption subsides, it is safe to return into the presence of the sensitive, damaged artist, I understand ...

Joe is now showing his need a bit

Joe Sarah, I only put that forward because I knew you'd be justifiably insecure.

Sarah (*realistically*) Work, Joe, I'll talk to you tonight about the play, I'm really thrilled for both of us, OK, tonight, bye ...

Joe (*quietly*) I need you ...

Sarah (*flashing with real anger*) Yeah, and I need me too! You men, you think if you say you need me or you love me that gives you rights, youthink somehow because *you* need me I have to come, that's not love, that's an *order*, did you think you could capture me with the play, eh, eh, Joe, you think I'm a fish, you put the play on a hook and dangle the line in the water and you can reel me in, did you, *wrong*, the question is *who* needs me, who is the whole you that needs me, and that's where *I* come in, that's where I choose, that's my rights. The one thing you did for me by throwing me out, you finally showed me *my* rights. Phone me at eight tonight, I have things to do, good morning! ... (*She puts down the phone and goes to get ready for work*) A caravan. It's gypsies now. A handicapped Jew isn't enough, gypsies ...

Joe sits. He neither paces nor sits in tension. He sits and thinks the whole thing over, and it is impossible to gauge his mood

Sarah has walked back, finishing her morning toilet

Joe thinks ...

Finally he goes to the phone and dials the fourteen numbers. But he makes a slip and so has to re-dial. This means replacing the receiver, waiting a few seconds, and re-dialling. He does this strongly, but with no extremes of emotion

It rings in Sarah's room. She sighs; it might be Joe, but she doesn't know, so answers "normally"

Sarah Hello?

Joe speaks with some force and great conviction, but not at all out of control; on the contrary, he has to make this count

Joe The play is not to trap you, it's not, that is *not* the meaning of the play. The fact that I can write the play and *give* you the play means that I have begun to accept that it wasn't a betrayal of my natural parents to love my American family and I don't any more have to destroy that happiness inside me. And that is why I can now love you and not have to throw you away, and *that* is the meaning of giving you the play.

Sarah hears in his voice the depth of this truth and feels and understands it, but also immediately knows that it is one-sided. She would love to give in, but ...

Sarah Joe, I can't. I can't, how do I know, it's just words, I don't trust it. Joe I love you, you have a friend for life, but I can't risk all that again ...

He speaks from a deep passion and place, deeper than the forgiving. But controlled

Joe But I have to trust you ... I have to trust you ... I have to trust that you don't fall down on this carpet and that I don't sit next to you in a hospital with tubes in your face and a man in a white coat tells me you're dead and I am again utterly, utterly alone, I have to trust that ...

She is silent

You risk a return flight home, but I risk that ... again. And I do risk it. I'll trust you for that, I'll risk it ...

There is a long, long pause. Sarah has been touched by a thought which simply never occurred to her—that there was any risk on the other side of such consequence. But she thinks. Joe waits. He has nothing else to say ...

Sarah Joe, have you heard of having goods on approval, do you have that over there?
Joe Yes.
Sarah OK. I'll make a deal with you, I'll make a deal with you, OK.
Joe Yes.
Sarah OK. I'll come over for a short stay. A trial. I'll take you on approval, I don't know how long, we'll see, I won't bring any books, I won't bring any records, just some clothes and we'll see, agreed? ...
Joe Yes.
Sarah You agree, you understand me?
Joe I do.
Sarah Second clause. Forget caravans, forget all thoughts and ideas of caravans, trailers, mobile homes, shelters for battered wives, forget it. If the Joe Green washing-machine runs down or explodes that's it, the Sarah Wise consumer group does *not mend motors*, agreed?
Joe (*sighing from tension*) Yes.
Sarah And understood.
Joe Yes, and understood.
Sarah OK. Clause three. If I get work over here, and I have a possible offer now, but whatever it is, it might even be your play, no explosions, no eruptions, I work. I'm lucky to get it, God damn it, is that also clear? Are all those points absolutely clear?
Joe I will put my signature between the two crosses in the appropriate place.
Sarah And understood.
Joe Yes.

A beat. Her tone is a touch kinder

Sarah In the marrow and in the bone.
Joe In the marrow and in the bone.

A beat. There is just a touch of lightness in her next condition, just a pinch

Sarah And there's a sub-clause, the small print. I'm handicapped, as you may have noticed, and even though I won't have that much hand-luggage, I'll need some help, so I want you to come out to the airport and meet me ...

Joe (*quietly; with a touch of a smile*) I'd rather you walked from the airport to me, if it's not too much trouble ...

Two beats. They stay on the phones a moment ...

The Lights fade to Black-Out

CURTAIN

FURNITURE AND PROPERTY LIST

JOE'S ROOM

On stage: Sofa. *On it:* cushions
Coffee table. *On it:* newspapers, letters, address book, cigarettes, lighter, pen, cheque book
Two armchairs
Round table. *On it:* typewriter, A4 paper, notes, pencil etc
Chairs around table
Bookshelves. *On them:* books, plays, photographs etc
Telephone on a long wire
Cuckoo clock on wall
Posters, watercolours on walls
Standard lamp
Carpet

SARAH'S ROOM

On stage: Double bed. *On it:* bedclothes, pillows. *By it:* crutches
Dressing table. *On it:* brushes, make-up etc
Bedside tables. *On one:* telephone, alarm clock, bedside light, aspirin, water
Oriental prints on wall
Bookcases
Curtains at window
Carpet

ACT I

Scene 1

On stage: Bowl of peaches on coffee table with spoon

Scene 2

Off stage: Glass of milk and biscuits **(Joe)**
Play copy **(Sarah)**

Scene 3

Off stage: Two plastic shopping bags **(Joe)**

Scene 4

Personal: **Sarah:** apple

SCENE 5

Set: Sunday papers on sofa
          Portable radio on coffee table

ACT II

SCENE 1

Off stage: Vacuum cleaner (practical) **(Joe)**

SCENE 2

          Tidy set
Set: Vase of flowers
Off stage: Mug of boiled water **(Joe)**
Personal: **Sarah:** coat, handbag, crutches
          Joe: cigarettes, lighter

SCENE 3

No props required

SCENE 4

No props required

SCENE 5

Off stage: Sarah's coat **(Joe)**
Personal: **Sarah:** handbag. *In it:* cassette

SCENE 6

No props required

SCENE 7

Off stage: Bowl of peaches and spoon **(Joe)**

LIGHTING PLOT

Two interior settings. Practical fittings required: standard lamp (Joe's room), bedside light (Sarah's room)

ACT I, SCENE 1

To open: Both areas lit

Cue 1	**Joe:** "... Mother, talk to me ..." *Fade to Black-Out*	(Page 7)

ACT I, SCENE 2

To open: Sarah's room dark with a shaft of light. Joe's room dark

Cue 2	When ready *Lights up in Joe's room*	(Page 7)
Cue 3	**Sarah** switches on light *Lights up in Sarah's room*	(Page 8)
Cue 4	**Both** put receivers down and think *Fade to Black-Out*	(Page 11)

ACT I, SCENE 3

To open: Morning light in both rooms

Cue 5	**Joe** exits, muttering a song *Fade to Black-Out*	(Page 16)

ACT I, SCENE 4

To open: Lights low in both rooms

Cue 6	**Joe** looks at his watch *Fade to Black-Out*	(Page 19)

ACT I, SCENE 5

To open: Sunshine

Cue 7	**Joe:** "Yes ..." Pause. When ready *Fade to Black-Out*	(Page 24)

ACT II, SCENE 1

To open: General lighting

Cue 8	**Joe** does karate chops *Fade to Black-Out*	(Page 30)

ACT II, SCENE 2

To open: Sarah's room dark, Joe's room in daylight

Cue 9	**Joe:** "... I can't get right, really ..." *Fade to Black-Out*	(Page 36)

ACT II, SCENE 3

To open: Darkness: moonlight or street light as appropriate

Cue 10	**Joe** turns on standard lamp *Snap on covering spot*	(Page 36)
Cue 11	**Joe** turns off lamp *Snap off lamp. Fade to Black-Out*	(Page 37)

ACT II, SCENE 4

To open: Darkness
No cues

ACT II, SCENE 5

To open: Lights up in Joe's room

Cue 12	**Sarah** waits *Fade to Black-Out*	(Page 41)

ACT II, SCENE 6

To open: Daylight

Cue 13	**Sarah:** "... happiness, anyway." (A beat) *Fade to Black-Out*	(Page 42)

ACT II, SCENE 7

To open: Morning light in both rooms

Cue 14	Two beats. They stay on the phones a moment *Fade to Black-Out*	(Page 49)

EFFECTS PLOT

ACT I

ACT II

Cue 17   **Joe** dials Sarah's number   (Page 42)
             Phone rings in Sarah's room

Cue 18   **Joe** fumbles for cheque book and pen   (Page 43)
             Sarah's alarm goes off

Cue 19   **Joe** dials a number (2nd time)   (Page 47)
             Phone rings in Sarah's room

MADE AND PRINTED IN GREAT BRITAIN BY
LATIMER TREND & COMPANY LTD PLYMOUTH

MADE IN ENGLAND